AMERICAN HISTORY:
Facts and Issues

by Matthew Testa

TBCB6-3

**DARNLEY
PUBLISHING
GROUP**

Legal deposit – Bibliothèque et Archives nationales du Québec, 2008
Legal deposit – Library and Archives Canada, 2008

ISBN 978-2-923623-41-2

Copyright © 2008 Darnley Publications Inc.

Printed in Canada

First Edition: 2008

TBCB6-3

Author:
Matthew Testa

Editor-In-Chief:
Claude Major, Ph.D.

Senior Editor:
Glen Speer, Ph.D.

Project Manager:
Francine Hebert, M.Ed.

Design and Cover:
Saskia Nieuwendijk
Rasha Razzak

Contributing Editors:
John McNeff
David Astroff
Michael Boulay
Jason Guzzo
Peter Richmond
Ray Staszko

SODEC
Québec ✚✚ Government of Quebec – Tax credit for book publishing – Administered by SODEC

TABLE OF CONTENTS

American History: Facts and Issues

Native Americans
Black Americans
First European Settlers
Westward Expansion
Waves of Immigration

Birth by Revolution
The War of 1812
Conflict with Native Americans
The Mexican-American War
The Civil War
The Spanish-American War
The World Wars
Korea and Vietnam

The Concept of Greatness
George Washington
Benjamin Franklin
Abraham Lincoln
Theodore Roosevelt
Woodrow Wilson
Franklin Roosevelt

No great man lives in vain. The history of the world is but the biography of great men.

THOMAS CARLYLE
1795-1881

INTRODUCTION

As compared to most other parts of the world, the United States as a country has a relatively brief history. Yet, in that comparatively short period of time, we have certainly been busy as a people, and have produced enough significant historical events to fill many volumes. Indeed, the study of American history is a specialized field to which many educators devote their entire lives.

As much as possible, this text is aimed at being both interesting and relevant to your life. The premise is to demonstrate that history is not just something that happened in the past, but rather consists of events that have made our world the way it is today. The realities with which we must cope in our society have historical roots. Without at least a brief understanding of these roots, people tend to misunderstand present day problems, oversimplifying them or incorrectly attributing their causes and solutions.

The subtitle of this text is "Facts and Issues." This simple phrase conveys an important point about history itself. Some people see history as merely a collection of facts and dates: George Washington was the first president of the country, the Civil War broke out in 1861, President Kennedy was assassinated in Dallas, Texas, in 1963. There is no end to the accumulation of names, dates, and statistics.

Facts can be defined — in theory — as information that is true and seldom disputed. In practice, however, some "facts" are very much in dispute. Still in debate, for example, is whether Lee Harvey Oswald acted alone in shooting President Kennedy or whether he was part of a larger conspiracy. Thus, who killed the president is a "fact" still open to debate. However, the time and place of his death are well accepted.

The term "issues," on the other hand, suggests that not all of history can be seen as black and white. We do not always agree on the causes or solutions to our problems. As a nation, we have argued over such issues as whether or not to go to war, how to punish criminals, and how or whether to promote equality within our society. Topics that transcend an isolated event and are open to debate and discussion are called issues. Sometimes, historical issues are far more interesting and important than the actual facts. Nonetheless, no study of history would be complete without an examination of both.

History itself, as a professional discipline, is a complex process. Historians frequently disagree with one another, not only about events and their interpretation, but about the process itself and its values. "Historiography" is a field devoted to the study of historians' various interpretations of history: how "the facts" change through the years, as our perspectives and values evolve.

Even a book that consists entirely of historical "facts" is never entirely neutral. There is still the matter of what facts to discuss and how to discuss them. In any history book, and particularly in a concise book such as this one, certain facts will receive less attention than those that are considered to be more important. Deciding on which topics to include or omit is tricky. In this text, we have selected some of the most important topics that every well-rounded American should know, as well as additional information on a few of the many great individuals and groups who have shaped the country as we know it today. There are of course many more stories to tell about American history, and we hope that this introductory text will inspire you to want to read more about them. Some suggestions for further reading are provided in the bibliography toward the end of this text.

It is also difficult to select what information to emphasize so the reader will be able to recall it later. Acquiring a basic knowledge of American history means more than simply memorizing a few dates. It means understanding some of the political, cultural, and economic contexts and causes of significant events. For example, "what caused the Civil War?" is in many ways a more important question than "when did the Civil War begin?" The first question, being about issues, is also more interesting because answering it requires an interpretation of the facts. Indeed, the facts are often easier to remember when you understand some of the issues that surround them.

Of course, you would not be considered a well-educated American if you were not familiar with some basic historical facts that should be common knowledge. You should know, for example, that the United States began as thirteen English colonies that united and declared their independence in 1776. You should know that George Washington was the commanding general of American forces during the Revolutionary War. You should know that Abraham Lincoln was president during the Civil War. You should know that Martin Luther King Jr. was an important leader of the civil rights movement in the 1950s and '60s that used nonviolent means to achieve equal rights for black Americans. These events occurred many years ago, but they are also examples of people and things that we as Americans continue to commemorate yet rarely stop to think about: the thirteen stripes on the American flag represent the original colonies, images of Washington and Lincoln are featured on our money, and King's birthday is a national holiday.

This book not only covers the essential facts about American history, but it also addresses some of the most fundamental issues. Chapter 1 examines who we are as a nation and where our ancestors came from. Because several wars were so important to the country's history, chapter 2 covers the major armed conflicts that the U.S. has participated in. Chapter 3 describes the background and achievements of America's greatest political leaders. Chapter 4 briefly explains how our government and civic life have evolved since independence. In chapter 5, we focus on the major events that have taken place since the end of World War II. Finally, chapter 6 introduces several notable civilian Americans and explains their lasting contributions to our society.

Because we live in a democratic society, as American citizens, we exert considerable power and influence over our leaders. When we cast our votes, we set in motion events that affect not only ourselves, but much of the rest of the world. It is unacceptable to undertake such significant actions in ignorance. If we do not understand our country thoroughly, then we cannot make wise and informed decisions about our present and our future.

CHAPTER ONE

WHO Are We?

A country is defined by its borders and geographic location, but much more so by its people. The roots of America are examined, from the early migration of Paleo-Indians to twentieth-century immigration trends.

LINCOLN MEMORIAL

Architect Henry Bacon modeled his design for the building after the Greek Parthenon. Built into the design are symbols like the 36 exterior Doric columns representing the 36 states in the Union at the time of Lincoln's death — the Union he had fought to preserve. Those states are listed on the frieze above the columns. Above those states are listed the 48 states in the Union when the memorial was built, making the memorial a tribute to the Union as much as a tribute to Lincoln himself. Alaska and Hawaii are represented with a plaque on the front steps.

America is God's Crucible, the great Melting-Pot where all the races of Europe are melting and reforming!

ISRAEL ZANGWILL
1864-1926

NATIVE AMERICANS

It would be a critical mistake to assume that American history began when the first Europeans sailed across the Atlantic Ocean and settled our shores. We now know that the first human beings (called Paleo-Indians) arrived on our continent at least 15,000 years ago and had spread throughout the Americas by 9000 BC. There is some debate over exactly when they arrived and exactly how they got here. One theory proposes they crossed over a land bridge from Siberia to Alaska where today there is only a narrow stretch of water between the continents. From there, they may have radiated southward and eastward, eventually dividing into groups that became separate from one another and evolved their own languages and cultures.

These are known as the native peoples of North America, or Native Americans, and they form the beginning of our history. You will find that it has not always been a pleasant history. The native peoples of North America still live in the United States and Canada. Their issues, problems, and concerns still challenge us as a society, and their culture and way of life

still fascinate and inspire us. These peoples were fundamental in establishing the basic spirit and framework for how we have come to see ourselves as a distinctive American culture.

Over many thousands of years, Native Americans would spread to every corner of North and South America and form unique tribes and civilizations. Native peoples studied nature and believed that they had a spiritual connection with the natural world. They cultivated maize (corn) and developed advanced agricultural societies.

The illustration on page 9 provides a brief summary of the names and main locations of Native Americans within the present United States and Canada. Because Native Americans are divided into so many distinct groups and there is lingering controversy about names or relationships among some groups, the following table is incomplete and numerous smaller groups are not mentioned. Also, the range of some groups extends beyond the states indicated and only the main areas are given.

Although the American Thanksgiving holiday celebrates, among other things, how Puritan settlers from England survived their first winter in America in 1620 with the help of the native peoples, by and large the history of interaction between whites and Native Americans has been a dark chapter in our history. It has involved confrontation, displacement, assimilation, segregation and the gradual loss of the native ways of life. While we cannot do justice to this complex subject here, an example is provided later in the text in the discussion of the life of Sitting Bull, one of many famous "Indian chiefs" who earned a lasting place in American history.

By the late 1800s and early 1900s, Native Americans across the continent were largely defeated, controlled, and segregated to living on "reserves" or "reservations." There, they experienced alienation from their traditional lifestyle and an array of social and economic problems. In recent years, however, there are some signs of hope that long-standing injustices may finally be set aright. Some tribes in the United States and Canada are now prospering under forms of limited self-government and a restitution of treaty rights originally extended to them but then violated. Still, many other bands live in acute poverty and there is much work to be done by their communities and by governments to continue and expand the progress. At one time, "progress" was defined as successful assimilation into white society. Today, the goal is rather to preserve the distinct character and traditions of the native peoples while allowing them full participation in American society to the extent that they desire it.

The first captives came to the Western Hemisphere in the early 1500s. Twenty African slaves were brought to Jamestown, Virginia, in 1619. A series of complex colonial laws began to relegate the status of Africans and their descendants to slavery. The United States outlawed the transatlantic slave trade, but slavery continued until 1865.

NATIVE-INDIAN - Regional Origins

Canadian Band Origins:

Inuit (formerly called Eskimo) — *broadly distributed across northern and northeastern territories;* *Mi'kmaq* — *Maritime provinces;* *Mohawk* — *Quebec, Ontario and southward into New York;* *Huron* — *Quebec and southward into U.S.;* *Ojibwa* — *Ontario, Manitoba and southward;* *Cree* — *Quebec west to Alberta;* *Blackfoot* — *Alberta and southward into U.S.*

NORTHWESTERN STATES
Salish Group

MONTANA
Blackfoot, Arapaho, Crow

DAKOTAS
Teton-Dakota, Crow (North)

GREAT LAKES REGION
Chippewa

NEW YORK
Iroquois Confederacy, Allegheny

WYOMING
Cheyenne

NEVADA
Shoshoni, Ute (Utah & Colorado)

ARIZONA
Apache, Mohave, Hopi

NEW MEXICO
Pueblo, Comanche (Texas)

SOUTHWEST
Navaho

MASSACH USETTS
Massachuset

TENNESSEE
Cherokee

FLORIDA
Seminole

CANADA

MIDWESTERN STATES

NORTHERN STATES

WESTERN STATES

UNITED STATES

North Pacific Ocean

North Atlantic Ocean

SOUTHERN STATES

CENTRAL PLAINS
Sioux

MEXICO

RUSSIA

HAWAII

ALASKA

CANADA

Gulf of Mexico

MISSISSIPPI
Choctaw

CUBA

Caribbean Sea

AFRICAN AMERICANS

Beginning in the sixteenth century, European traders bought or kidnapped Africans to import to the New World and be used for slave labor. In the North American colonies, slaves worked mainly on tobacco and cotton plantations in the American south, and they and their descendents continued to work on southern farms until slavery was finally outlawed after the Civil War, in 1865.

The plight of blacks under slavery will be discussed later in the text, in tracing the foundations of the Civil War. The ongoing struggle of black Americans for equality and fair treatment is described in the section profiling Martin Luther King.

The legacy of slavery and the widespread discrimination against blacks that followed it are shameful parts of America's history. Although progress has been made in recent decades to promote racial equality, there is still much work to be done.

FIRST EUROPEAN SETTLERS

England founded the colony of Virginia in 1607. For about the next 160 years, England would acquire or establish many more colonies in North America. The thirteen colonies that eventually became the first American states stretch from New Hampshire in the north to Georgia in the south. These colonies attracted not only English settlers, but also French, German, Dutch, Swedish, Scottish, Irish, Jewish, and other European settlers.

The settlers brought their European culture with them, some of which continues to shape American culture. The Puritans who settled New England valued a high work ethic—a belief that work is morally redeeming. Because many settlers came to colonial America to escape religious persecution, the principle of freedom of religion also came to be prized. And, of course, one of the most enduring aspects of the colonial era is language: the U.S. would not be an English-speaking nation today if some other European power had settled here!

WESTWARD EXPANSION

After the original thirteen states, the rest of the country grew gradually over the years as a result of a complex pattern of settlements and treaties. From the beginning, the United States expected to grow and planned for this growth. A process was established whereby newly settled or acquired land would be set up as a "territory" administered by the federal government. When its population and development reached a certain level, the territory could apply for statehood. Thus, by looking at the dates in which states were formally admitted to the Union, the westward expansion of the nation can roughly be charted. As can be seen from the dates listed on page 12, the growth of the country wasn't an orderly movement from east

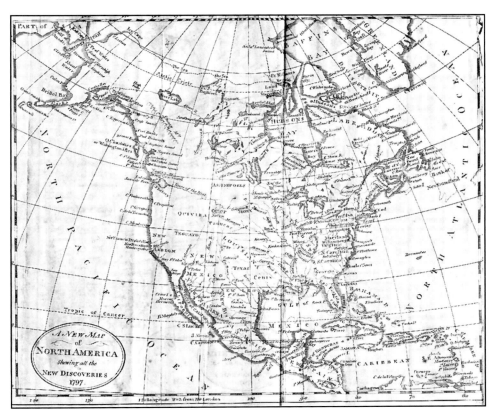

This original map appears in The American Gazetter published by Jedidiah Morse in 1797. The map, specially engraved for the country's first geographical dictionary, shows a relatively accurate physical outline of North America, providing students of this era with a valuable historical marker.

to west. Some areas, especially on the west coast, were settled and achieved statehood well before areas farther east — meaning that, at one time, the country contained large gaps of territory which had not yet achieved statehood.

WAVES OF IMMIGRATION

The U.S. is known as a nation of immigrants, a nation that has often—though not always—welcomed people from foreign lands. In practice, however, that welcome has often wavered in enthusiasm. Many nationalities were slow to be accepted upon first arriving, and were often relegated to menial occupations, only "assimilating" gradually over time. Some groups faced racial or ethnic and religious discrimination upon arriving here. This was sometimes fueled by prejudice, but economic factors also played a role. Especially in times of economic recession, many Americans fear competition from immigrants in landing jobs. Immigrants have also fared poorly here during periods when America was at war with their

STATEHOOD
By Date

Delaware	1787	Michigan	1837
Pennsylvania	1787	Florida	1845
New Jersey	1787	Texas	1845
Georgia	1788	Iowa	1846
Connecticut	1788	Wisconsin	1848
Massachusetts	1788	California	1850
Maryland	1788	Minnesota	1858
South Carolina	1788	Oregon	1859
New Hampshire	1788	Kansas	1861
Virginia	1788	West Virginia	1863
New York	1788	Nevada	1864
North Carolina	1789	Nebraska	1867
Rhode Island	1790	Colorado	1876
Vermont	1791	North Dakota	1889
Kentucky	1792	South Dakota	1889
Tennessee	1796	Montana	1889
Ohio	1803	Washington	1889
Louisiana	1812	Idaho	1890
Indiana	1816	Wyoming	1890
Mississippi	1817	Utah	1896
Illinois	1818	Oklahoma	1907
Alabama	1819	New Mexico	1912
Maine	1820	Arizona	1912
Missouri	1821	Alaska	1959
Arkansas	1836	Hawaii	1959

NOTE:

The first thirteen states—the original colonies—became states upon ratifying the Constitution. However, they were also considered states previous to this under the Articles of Confederation.

homeland. This was especially true of Japanese-Americans during World War II. While our record on immigration is hardly an unblemished one, by comparison with other nations we are a culture of diverse peoples in which we are protected under the law from discrimination based on race, language, or religion.

While immigration has proceeded steadily throughout our history, with a few gaps when it was severely restricted, there were certain times in which larger "waves" of people immigrated from a specific country. The following section provides a brief summary of some of these major immigration patterns. While it is not possible to mention all nationalities here, the examples provided give a general idea of the types of forces that propelled people to seek a life in a new world.

French — Most French immigration predated the formation of the United States as an

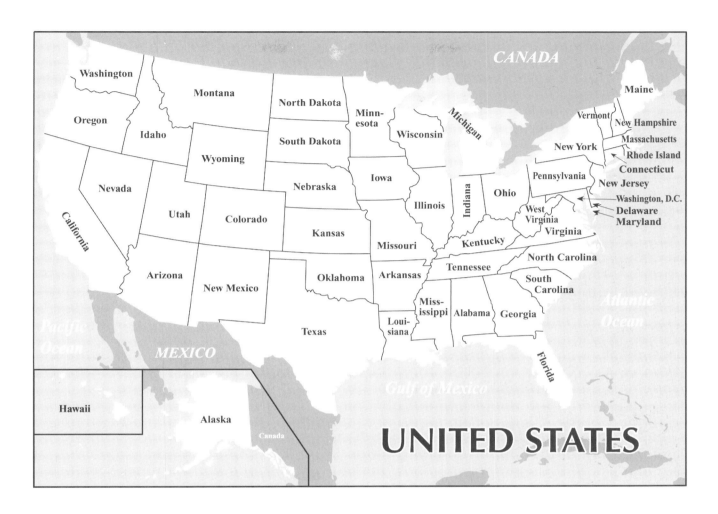

UNITED STATES

independent country. French Huguenots were forced to leave France in the seventeenth century, and many came to America. They settled Quebec, fanned westward into the area surrounding the Great Lakes, charted and explored the central third of the country, and began important settlements in Louisiana, which preserves a French character to this day.

Scottish — Protestant Scots settled in Northern Ireland and lived there for centuries, but by the early 1700s they faced persecution. Many emigrated to the colonies, settling in rural parts of Virginia, the Carolinas, and western Pennsylvania.

Irish — Irish Catholics began coming to America in the early 1700s. Between 1845 and 1900, 3.5 million Irish people settled in America, many of them fleeing from starvation. Because they were Catholics coming to a largely Protestant land, they suffered considerable discrimination in many areas until their sheer numbers helped give them political power in the big cities. By the 1880s, they dominated the politics of much of the east, midwest, and parts of California.

British — In addition to the original colonists, people from England, Scotland, and Wales continued to immigrate to the United States.

Because of their cultural similarity to Americans, they were one of the few groups that was easily assimilated and never faced significant prejudice.

Germans — Europe was rapidly changing in the mid-1800s, due to political revolution, and it was not always a smooth or pleasant process. In 1848, many Germans were exiled for political reasons, and over 4 million immigrated to the United States by the turn of the century. Unlike many other groups, the Germans often came with enough money to purchase land right away, and many moved to the midwest where they could acquire farmland cheaply. Large groups of German Americans remain in many areas including Wisconsin, Missouri, and Texas. There was also a prominent German population in New York City.

Chinese — While many groups faced opposition or practical problems upon first arriving in America, the plight of the nineteenth century Chinese immigrants was especially unfortunate. Many fled overpopulation and famine in China, taking over menial jobs when they settled, mainly in California. Their labor was exploited profitably by many American business tycoons, in particular to work on the transcontinental railroad. But when the west lapsed into an economic depression in 1873, the Chinese immigrants were often blamed. They were then subjected to unfair and discriminatory laws that slowed their immigration (in particular, the Chinese Exclusion Act, which remained in force from 1882 to 1892). The Chinese also suffered because they were so culturally different from Americans that suspicions and misunderstandings were all the more likely. For

these reasons, they tended to cluster together in isolated communities which became the "Chinatowns" of many western American cities. When, like other groups, they eventually won greater tolerance and acceptance, they spread to other parts of the country.

Jews — By 1880, there were roughly 150,000 German Jews settled in the United States. Most were tradesmen or businessmen. Although they held fast to their religious heritage, on the whole they quickly adopted American customs. There were also smaller numbers of Jews of Spanish and Portuguese (Sephardic) descent who settled in Rhode Island, New York, Charleston, Savannah, and New Orleans. Again, the original Jewish settlers were reasonably well-off and well-received. There was also a great wave of Eastern European Jews from 1880 to 1920. When the Jewish people began to be persecuted in Nazi Germany and other parts of Europe in the 1930s, large numbers came to the United States under less ideal circumstances. Many Jews couldn't get here because of our strict immigration laws at that time. Here, Jews often faced, and sometimes continue to face, discrimination. However, America was generally sympathetic to their plight after the Second World War, and continues to be a close ally of Israel. Jewish Americans are prominent in virtually all aspects of American life today.

Filipinos — By the end of the nineteenth century, Filipinos and Japanese had become the main groups of Asian immigrants. Filipinos had relatively easy access to the U.S. after their country was annexed as a territory by the U.S. Congress.

Japanese — Originally, Japanese immigrants entered the U.S. mainly through Hawaii, where they were an important factor in the agricultural workforce. They came to face much of the same discrimination and resentment the Chinese faced, though their immigration was not severely restricted until the mid-1920s, a time during which most other immigrant groups, except northern Europeans, were also shut out.

Although their immigration was spread over a longer period of time, America has also welcomed large numbers of people from Italy, Poland, Saudi Arabia and other countries in the Middle East, India and Pakistan, Mexico, and Puerto Rico (which is a U.S. territory).

In modern times, immigration to the U.S. has been strictly controlled under a system that, at least in theory, attempts to grant fair access to people from all parts of the world. Priority is also given to refugees fleeing from documented political persecution. There were,

for example, large influxes of Koreans during and after the Korean Conflict and of Vietnamese after the war in Vietnam.

There have always been a great many more people in the world wanting to come to this country than could be absorbed socially or economically. As a result, some restrictions on immigration remain a necessity. We vary from one administration or congressional session to another in our relative openness to increasing or decreasing the flow, but it is doubtful that the United States — a nation of immigrants— will ever close its doors entirely to the people of the world who dream of one day joining and participating in our society, with its freedom and potential for prosperity and personal achievement. However, upon arriving here, many have found the welcome not as enthusiastic as they had expected, and the struggle to find employment and adapt to the American lifestyle was often more difficult than they had anticipated.

Chapter One • Recap Quiz

1. Which present-day American state was probably first visited by the first Paleo-Indians who took the "landbridge" route to the North American continent?

2. Name a group of North American Indians that is primarily associated with the Great Lakes area.

3. What two states were the last to enter the Union and complete our present-day 50 states?

4. Which group of immigrants was particularly instrumental in building the western portion of the transcontinental railroad?

5. Name a group of immigrants that had comparatively easy access to America after their homeland was annexed by the U.S.?

Answers to quiz one

1- Alaska   2- Chippewa   3- Alaska and Hawaii   4- Chinese   5- Filipinos

CHAPTER TWO

AMERICA
at War

From its birth by
revolution to the
complex lessons of Vietnam,
America has a history
that is marked
by war.

ARLINGTON NATIONAL CEMETERY

Arlington National Cemetery, United States federal burial ground in northeastern Virginia, is administered by the Department of the Army. The site, on the Potomac River across from Washington, D.C., occupies more than 612 acres and contains the remains of more than 240,000 veterans, their dependents, and political leaders.

The use of force alone is but temporary. It may subdue for a moment; but it does not remove the necessity of subduing again; and a nation is not governed, which is perpetually to be conquered.

EDMUND BURKE
1729-1797

Victory at all costs, victory in spite of terror, victory however long and hard the road may be; for without victory there is no survival.

SIR WINSTON CHURCHILL
1874-1965

There never was a good war, or a bad peace.

BENJAMIN FRANKLIN
1706-1790

BIRTH BY REVOLUTION

America's first war as a nation was that which gave birth to it, the Revolutionary War, which began in 1775. Thirteen colonies of Great Britain united to form the United States of America. These colonies stretched from New Hampshire to Georgia along the East Coast of the country. By and large, they were all settled by British descendants, although isolated groups of other European descent were also living in our cities.

The colonial system was complex. In those days, Great Britain and several other world powers maintained colonies in several parts of the world. Essentially, the colonies existed to create wealth for the mother country. Thus, the people living in the colonies were subjects of the king, but they generally lacked the privileges of people living in the mother country. For example, although Britain was already moving toward a parliamentary system of government, the American colonies had no significant voice in the British parliament. Even though the colonies had their own legislature, many of the important laws that were made with respect to the colonies were made in England without the consent of the colonists.

The colonial situation was nonetheless different from that of a conquered territory. Since most of the people living in America at that time (not including Native Americans or the black slaves who had been brought to southern colonies from Africa) were of British descent, they did not necessarily feel hostile towards Britain. In fact, many historians describe the American Revolution as a type of

No Stamped Paper to be had.

BOSTON, October 28.

WE hear from Halifax, in the province of Nova-Scotia, that on Sunday, the 13th inst. in the morning, was discovered hanging on the gallows behind the Citadel Hill, the effigies of a stampman, accompanied with a boot and devil, together with labels suitable to the occasion (which we cannot insert, not being favoured with the same) this we are informed gave great pleasure and satisfaction to all the friends of liberty and their country there, as they hope from this instance of their zeal, the neighbouring colonies will be charitable enough to believe that nothing but their dependent situation, prevents them from heartily and sincerely opposing a tax unconstitutional in its nature, and of so destructive a tendency as must infallibly entail poverty and beggary on us and our posterity, if carried in execution.

On the 23d instant the Great and General Court met here, according to adjournment; and we hear that almost every member of the honourable house of representatives have received instructions from their constituents; and that they are of the same import with those already published.

We hear that the merchants and friends to America in England, were determined to use their utmost endeavours the next session of Parliament, in order to get the stamp act repealed.

NEW-YORK, November 4.

The late extraordinary and unprecedented preparations in Fort George, and the securing of the stamped paper in that garrison, having greatly alarmed and displeased the inhabitants of this city, a vast number of them assembled last Friday evening in the commons, from whence they marched down the Fly (preceded by a number of lights) and having stopped a few minutes at the Coffee-house, proceeded to the Fort walls, where they broke open the stable of the L———t G———r, took out his coach, and after carrying the same through the principal streets of the city, in triumph marched to the commons, where a gallows was erected ; on one end of which was suspended the effigy of the person whose

George the Third, to the crown of Great-Britain, &c. upon which occasion the said freemen unanimously, and with one voice declared,

First. That they have at all times heretofore, and ever would bear true allegiance to his Majesty King George the Third, and his royal predecessors, and wished to be governed agreeable to the laws of the land, and the British constitution, to which they ever had, and for ever most chearfully would submit.

Secondly. That the stamp act, prepared for the British colonies in America, in their opinion, is unconstitutional; and should the same take place, agreeable to the tenor of it, would be a manifest destruction and overthrow of their long enjoyed, boasted and invaluable liberties and privileges.

Thirdly. That they will, by all lawful ways and means, endeavour to preserve and transmit to posterity, their liberty and property, in as full and ample manner as they received the same from their ancestors.

Fourthly. That they will discountenance and discourage, by all lawful measures, the execution and effect of the stamp act.

Fifthly. That they will detest, abhor, and hold in the utmost contempt, all and every person or persons, who shall meanly accept of any employment or office, relating to the stamp act, or shall take any shelter or advantage from the same ; and all and every stamp pimp, informer, favourer and encourager of the execution of the said act ; and that they will have no communication with any such person, nor speak to them on any occasion, unless it be to inform them of their vileness.

CITY of NEW-YORK, October 31, 1765.

AT a general Meeting of the Merchants of the City of New-York, trading to Great-Britain, at the House of Mr. George Burns, of the said City, Innholder, to consider what was necessary to be done in the present Situation of Affairs, with respect to the STAMP ACT, and the melancholy State of the North-American Commerce, so greatly restricted by the Impositions and Duties established by the late Acts of Trade: They came to the following Resolutions, viz.

First, That in all Orders they send out to Great-Britain, for Goods or Merchandize, of any Nature, Kind or Quality whatsoever, usually imported from Great-Britain, they will direct their Correspondents not to ship them, unless the STAMP Act be repealed: It is nevertheless agreed, that all such Merchants as are Owners of, and have Vessels already gone, and now cleared out for Great-Britain, shall be at Liberty to bring back in them, on their own Accounts, Crates and Casks of Earthen Ware, Grindstones, Pipes, and such other bulky Articles, as Owners usually fill up their Vessels with.

Nov. 7, 1765, issue no. 1924, of the Pennsylvania Gazette, printed at Philadelphia by David Hall and Benjamin Franklin; without date, number, masthead, or imprint. On Oct. 31, 1765, the publishers announced the suspension of the Gazette in opposition to the provisions of the Stamp Act, which required that newspapers be printed on imported, stamped paper. By issuing sheets without the characteristic appearance of the newspaper they were able to satisfy the subscribers while protecting the firm from legal repercussions.

civil war between colonists who rebelled and colonists who remained loyal to England. Even when the revolution began, a considerable portion of the population (estimated to be one-fifth) opposed the revolutionary leaders. After the war was over, many of these loyalists moved north to Canada, which remained under British control. (Canada did not become an independent nation until much later in its history.)

The issue that finally provoked the American Revolution had less to do with a desire for nationhood than with a frustration over taxes and other measures that made colonists feel they were being exploited by the British. The colonies were a rich source of raw materials, cloth, food, tobacco, and other commodities. As more and more people moved to America from Europe, the rapidly swelling population created a significant tax base. The British, who at the time were engaged in small wars in other parts of the world, needed to restock their treasury with tax dollars, as well as get necessary supplies and raw materials as cheaply as possible. Various measures were taken that angered the colonists. The Stamp Act, which imposed a tax on all documents and newspapers, was among the most notorious. The colonists began to feel that they were being unfairly exploited and overtaxed by a government that would not listen to their concerns or afford them the respect that they were due as British subjects.

The colonists' building frustration and anger toward Britain led at first to defiance of new taxes and of the so-called Intolerable Acts. In one famous incident, the Boston Tea Party, colonial rebels dumped forty-five tons of

Cornwallis and the British Army surrendered on October 19, 1781, in Yorktown, Virginia.

British tea into the Boston harbor to protest new limitations on what tea could be sold. As politicians of colonies organized a Continental Congress to find a diplomatic solution, militias in each of the colonies assembled and prepared to fight. Battles first erupted in Massachusetts in 1775 and then spread into New England and elsewhere. Britain wanted to crush the rebellion and keep the colonies until their control. Consequently, they sent over all divisions of the British army and navy which could be spared in order to subdue the rebels among the colonists and restore peace and order. In doing so, however, they seriously underestimated the opposition they would face or how difficult it would be to defeat the insurrectionists.

The American patriots, as they now called themselves, had other ideas. Under General George Washington, the colonies managed to muster a significant army and sufficient supplies to keep it minimally functional. The Continental Army was a poor man's army, and at first it was in disarray. It suffered particularly

during the winter months when there was relatively little fighting and it was difficult to keep the army going without adequate food, clothing, and shelter.

The American forces had some advantages over the British, despite being underfinanced and underprovisioned, not to mention lacking in military training. That they were fighting on their home soil was clearly an advantage. The British troops were so far from home that keeping them well-supplied and even keeping the lines of communication in order was a difficult task.

Moreover, most of the patriots fighting were militia members who could be assembled at a moment's notice ("minutemen"), not professional soldiers who had much formal military training or even uniforms. Thus the patriots had to rely on guerrilla tactics.

Before the American Revolution, it was common for armies to march into battle wearing bright uniforms, stand in straight lines

The "original Rough draught" of the Declaration of Independence, one of the great milestones in American history, shows the evolution of the text from the initial "fair copy" draft by Thomas Jefferson to the final text adopted by Congress on the morning of July 4, 1776. (See appendix C.)

and fire upon one another in the open, leaving it to fate, marksmanship, and courage as to which army prevailed. The American revolutionaries realized that they had little chance of victory by using traditional methods of fighting. Consequently, they adopted another strategy. Rather than confronting the enemy in the open on the battlefield, they often used stealth, hiding behind bushes and trees and attacking troops by surprise in order to inflict heavy casualties and cause confusion and demoralization.

From the American point of view, the morality of this new style of fighting was easily justified. The patriots were fighting for their homeland and for their freedom.

After five years of on-and-off fighting, this strategy, coupled with some poor decisions by the British generals, led to the surrender of British General Cornwallis at Yorktown, Virginia. No war is ever a simple event, and without detailing the entire history of this war — which would take a book in itself — we can detail its complexity by mentioning that Cornwallis tried to snub Washington by surrendering to the French, who had aided the patriots, rather than to the despised "Americans." The surrender at Yorktown stopped the fighting and led to an uneasy and uncertain state of affairs that wasn't resolved until almost two years later, when the Treaty of Paris settled outstanding issues, such as the boundary between the United States and Canada.

The American system of government that emerged was unique and has proven to be one of the most innovative and important institutions in human history. Although some token form of democracy began to appear in England and in a few other places, the type of democracy found in the United States, where (eventually) all citizens were deemed equal regardless of wealth or class, was quite novel. The founding fathers of our country established a complex system of government that was accountable to the citizenry, who elected representatives on a regular basis.

A significant point to grasp is that the American system of government was new and it sparked the imagination of other countries. Our revolution, which was originally inspired in part by thinkers in France and Scotland, indirectly inspired the French Revolution, which overthrew the French monarchy and established the first form of democracy in that country. However, democracy was still a risky experiment, and for many years after the end of the Revolutionary War, its survival in the U.S. was by no means secure and assured, since the nation's abilities to govern and defend its territory were still questionable.

Many would argue that the British did more to lose the Revolutionary War than our leaders actually did to win it. However, the emergence of our system of government was the true victory that General Washington extracted from our country's first and perhaps most significant armed conflict.

Unfortunately, the high ideals of "life, liberty and the pursuit of happiness" extended only to white male citizens of the country, not to women, the Native Americans, or the slaves. From the beginning, the liberty and virtue of our nation were marred by this inconsistency. It would take several other armed conflicts and more than a hundred years before some of these contradictions would be resolved.

THE WAR OF 1812

When the British conceded defeat at the end of the American Revolution, they did not entirely dismiss the possibility of one day reasserting control over the colonies. Only the colonies that formed the original states passed out of British control. Britain maintained other colonies, particularly to the north in territories which have since become Canada. Britain was not ready to leave the continent altogether, and the presence of British colonies on the doorstep of the new American nation was bound to be an ongoing source of conflict.

This conflict finally erupted most dramatically in what became known as the War of 1812. This war is one of the murkiest, least clearly understood chapters in America's military history, and it can only be given a brief mention in a summary presentation such as this one. Unlike most wars, it was more a series of isolated scrimmages between various factions which included Americans, British forces, French Canadians, and various Indian nations. It started over frustration with British interference with American shipping and British-Canadian assistance to Native American Indians who were in constant conflict with U.S. settlers in the Midwest and northwestern territories.

Were it not for the tragedy of destruction and loss of life, it would be possible to write the script of this war as a "black comedy." Both sides were often militarily inept and quarreled among themselves. Shortly after an American force captured York (now Toronto) and burned several government buildings, a rogue band of British troops launched an amphibious raid on Washington, D.C. There, they nearly captured President Madison, enjoyed a dinner that had been cooked for him, and set fire to the White House and the Capitol—a cause of much future Anglo-American ill will.

In the early days of the war, Britain was inhibited by its more significant war against Napoleon and the French in Europe and in the Caribbean. Once Napoleon was defeated, the British briefly entertained the idea of seizing Louisiana from the United States. This led to one of the few truly impressive military victories of the war: Andrew Jackson's defeat of the British at the Battle of New Orleans in 1815. Ironically, it took place two weeks after a peace treaty had been signed.

In the end, relatively little was accomplished. Everyone more or less went back to where they had been living in the first place and agreed for the time being to respect each other's boundaries and leave one another alone. However, this in itself was no small achievement for the new nation. At that time, America was hardly a world power. Our independence was only as secure as our ability to defend it, and with other countries having their eyes on us, it was doubtful whether the new nation could go on for much longer without another attempt to conquer it. In the War of 1812, America so demonstrated its tenacity and determination to protect its existence that the British never again mounted a serious attempt to reacquire their original colonies, although many times Britain and the U.S. almost went to war again. Within a relatively short period of time, Britain and America were beginning to show signs of cooperation. The

weakening of the power of the monarchy in Britain had a lot to do with making this possible. In a much slower and more roundabout way, by 1832 Britain had also transformed itself into a limited democracy.

From then on, rapid growth and expansion within America made it less and less of an easy target for any foreign power. We were never again seriously challenged by an invading army determined to make us their colony.

CONFLICT WITH NATIVE AMERICANS

Until recently, many textbooks on American history jumped from the War of 1812 to the American Civil War to the Spanish American War, failing to mention several decades of almost continuous battles between white Americans and the Native Americans, then called the "Indians." One reason that these conflicts received relatively little mention is because they tended to be very complex in nature, mainly isolated attacks on individual bands and counterattacks by the native peoples. There was not a unified series of related activities that could easily be termed a "war" in the conventional sense.

Another reason for glossing over this chapter in our history is that it is not a particularly pretty one. Although, at the time, Native Americans were portrayed to the public as barbarians with a thirst for blood and little sense of morality and decency, we now know that this was not true. The American settlers pushing westward, and the American Army

Sitting Bull (1831?-1890), Native American leader of the Sioux, born in the region of the Grand River in present-day South Dakota. Led by Sitting Bull, the Sioux resisted efforts of the United States government to annex their lands and force them to settle on reservations. Between June 25 and June 26, 1876, the Sioux, with the aid of other tribes, annihilated a punitive expedition commanded by Lieutenant Colonel George Armstrong Custer in the Battle of Little Bighorn.

which accompanied them to ensure their safety, were often the aggressors in these conflicts. Certainly, there were atrocities on both sides, but it is clear that Native Americans, often with good reason, perceived themselves as under attack and defending their homeland, and saw the American settlers as the invaders.

The settlers also caused the destruction of buffalo herds upon which many of the tribes depended. Thus, much as the American revolutionaries justified their tactics because they felt they were defending their homeland, Native Americans felt much the same way.

Although Native Americans managed some significant and dramatic victories during these many armed struggles — the defeat of General Custer in the Battle of Little Bighorn in 1876 being the most famous one — by and large the Native Americans were systematically defeated, pushed back, and gradually placed under the control of the U.S. federal government. As America expanded westward, it claimed more and more territory. Eventually, as one group or another of Native Americans were defeated or driven out, treaties were signed relegating them to reservations and limiting their freedom within what was then perceived as a U.S. territory in the making.

While much of this was going on, the other unpleasant aspect of early American society, slavery, was gradually propelling us towards our most traumatic and bloody war of all time: the American Civil War, fought between 1861 and 1865. Before turning to that conflict, however, there was one other neighbor with whom America seemed fated to enter into conflict: Mexico.

THE MEXICAN-AMERICAN WAR

The Mexican-American War of 1846, and the various battles that preceded it ten years earlier, form an interesting chapter of American

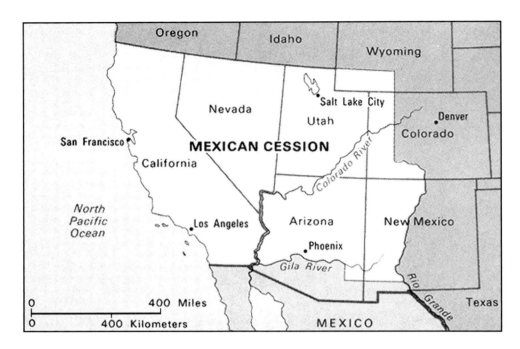

MEXICAN-AMERICAN WAR

In 1845 the United States annexed the Republic of Texas, which had recently won its independence from Mexico. Tension between the United States and Mexico mounted following a dispute over the location of the Texas border. This dispute led to the Mexican-American War (1846-1848). At the conclusion of the war, Mexico ceded a large tract of territory that comprises much of what is now the southwestern United States.

history, but one that is sometimes overlooked. The Mexican War is fascinating because it serves as a model for understanding the majority of wars that have taken place throughout world history. Reduced to its simplest, though admittedly oversimplified terms, the Mexican War was a result of what happens when two different peoples with two different cultures try to settle the same piece of land.

After the Mexican War, the area that now comprises Texas, Arizona, New Mexico and California were poised to eventually become part of the United States. However, Americans were actually the third people to settle this territory. The Native Americans were the first, of course, settling thousands of years before the first Europeans. The first persons of European descent to move into this territory were the Spanish, and more specifically the Spanish-speaking Mexicans. While there was a

long history of tension between the English and the Spanish for many centuries, and some tensions between the American colonies and Spain, Mexico was independent of Spain by 1821 and initially looked to become allied with the United States.

At first, the Americans who moved into some of Mexico's northern territories were welcome. The land which would soon be in dispute between the two countries was relatively far from the main centers of the Mexican population. As such, it functioned almost like a Mexican province. The residents suffered some disadvantages in regard to trade, and some of their economic problems were more easily remedied by looking to trade with the Americans rather than with the Mexicans. One of the first such trade routes was established between Missouri and Santa Fe (the Santa Fe Trail), then a Mexican settlement, though one with a vibrant Spanish-Indian culture and a population of Spanish Jews.

This was followed by a formal invitation, extended by the Mexicans, for American settlers to move into portions of Texas. The settlers signed an agreement promising to abide by Mexican law, to learn the Spanish language and to practice the Roman Catholic religion which was fundamental throughout the Spanish-speaking world. Like many settlement schemes, it began with good intentions but then grew in proportions that the original government officials never intended.

When General Antonio Lopez de Santa Anna came to power in Mexico in 1833, relations with Americans in northern Mexican territories rapidly began to sour. As the privileges of both Mexican and American settlers in Texas were restricted, an uprising, somewhat similar to the uprising that had fueled the original American Revolution, seemed inevitable for many of the same reasons.

A complex and muddled sequence of events then followed. American settlers in Texas defied Santa Anna and began to move for independence. Santa Anna became determined to crush them with military force. In 1836 he attacked a relatively insignificant garrison in Texas called the Alamo. Though its Texan defenders had no chance to withstand Santa Anna's siege, they continued to struggle stubbornly. In the end, not only was the Alamo captured by Santa Anna, but all of the prisoners, including many women, were executed. Though this move was not entirely without military precedent in Spanish history,

Santa Anna did his cause far more harm than good with the executions, as he fermented a hatred against him which further fueled the drive for Texan independence. "Remember the Alamo" became a rallying cry.

Santa Anna then continued his campaign in Rio San Jacinto, where he was defeated and captured by Sam Houston. Though Santa Anna would later repudiate it, he was forced to recognize the Republic of Texas as an independent country.

Almost immediately, the Lone Star Republic of Texas began to look to merge with the United States. However, for various reasons, not the least of which was the fact that Texas had legalized slavery, there was opposition in the American Congress. For a while, the frustrated Texans tried to seek an alliance with the British, although, once again, slavery became an obstacle. In 1837, a widespread economic depression in the United States focused attention away from all the territorial squabbles along its western boundaries and the question of Texas remained in limbo for a time.

By the election of 1844, the debate over the annexation of Texas had become the main political issue. By then, there was a significant contingent within America that favored the doctrine of Manifest Destiny, a belief that America was destined by God to eventually occupy the North American continent from sea to sea. This seemed to make the annexation of Texas essential, and attention was also focused on settlements in California and the land in between the two. The new president, James Polk, made it the primary mission of his presidency to secure Texas and other western territory. Almost immediately, difficulties with the Mexicans became the inevitable result.

By this time, General Santa Anna was back in power in Mexico. Perhaps he had learned some lessons from the days of the Alamo, for at first he proceeded cautiously. The aggressor in the situation was clearly Polk, who thought he could win a war and clearly wanted to provoke one. He launched an offensive into a disputed region under the command of General Zachary Taylor. Taylor, together with General Winfield Scott, then undertook a series of campaigns which resulted in a relatively straightforward and systematic defeat of the Mexican forces, culminating in the occupation of Mexico City and the Treaty of Guadalupe Hidalgo in 1848.

The primary result of this treaty was that huge portions of Mexican territory were ceded to the United States. Although money was paid to the Mexicans for much of this territory, it was clearly a stunning defeat for Mexico and the end of what opportunity it might have had to remain a strong economic and military force in North America.

The Mexican-American War had been particularly popular among most Americans for a variety of reasons. They liked the idea of the new territories that their expanding country would now have access to. They enjoyed the relatively steady stream of military successes. However, there were a few politicians within the country who felt that, despite Polk's rhetoric, the American forces had been the wrongful aggressors in the situation. Many

northerners also worried that slavery would spread into the new territory. For this reason, one of the young politicians who had voted against the declaration of war was an Illinois congressman named Abraham Lincoln, who would soon become involved in a war with much more disastrous consequences.

THE CIVIL WAR

In a previous section of this text, we referred to the early history of black Americans and the circumstances involved in their being brought from Africa as slaves. Slavery was, at least on the surface, the primary issue which triggered the American Civil War in 1861. However, the events leading up to the war are exceedingly complex and go back several decades over an uneasy period in American history where tensions between North and South were steadily fermenting.

In the early and middle 1800s, the cultural and economic differences between the northern and southern states were already so great that, to many, they probably appeared to be two separate nations. Southerners identified themselves as Southerners before they identified themselves as Americans. The economy of the South was built entirely around agriculture and shipping. The economy of the North was more diversified and was already entering the early phases of the Industrial Revolution.

All of the large American cities were located in the North, with the exception of New Orleans. By 1860, there were over 800,000 people in New York City and over

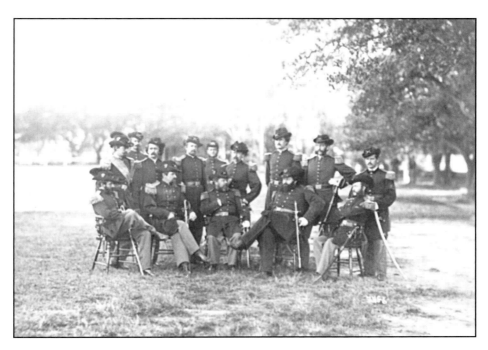

Officers of 3d Pennsylvania Heavy Artillery, Fort Monroe, Virginia.

500,000 in Philadelphia. Although New Orleans had 168,000, each of the cities of Charleston, Richmond, Mobile, and Memphis had fewer than 40,000 residents. By today's standards, they wouldn't even be considered large towns.

The wealth of the South lay mainly in the hands of a relatively few plantation owners. As such, the economic and political system of the South resembled that of Europe, where barons or lords owned large tracts of land and lived in mansions or castles while the vast majority were poor, oppressed laborers who owned very little. In the American South, slavery made this possible. In theory, the South was every bit a part of the United States as the rest of the country, and the United States was a democracy where every man had a vote. However, in practice, the slaves had no political power whatsoever. Even female members of the upper classes were not allowed to vote. Poor white citizens, if they did vote, were apt to vote as they were told by the powerful and influential men who had the ability to hire and fire, to make work or take it away.

Today, it is difficult for many people to understand how a democratic country, and a Christian one, could have allowed such situations to develop. There is no universal agreement on this issue. However, some would argue that, to some extent, Christianity actually played a role in perpetuating this system. Many

Whitehall Street in Atlanta, Georgia, shortly after the forced retreat of the Confederates in 1864.

white Southerners, even those who were kindly and generous by inclination and devoted to their faith, believed that the black race was inferior, that slavery was a "positive good," and that it was God's will that blacks be controlled by whites so that they could be introduced to Christianity and the American view of law and morality. Many mistook lack of education for lack of intelligence. Certainly, the only education the slaves received was often that which they arranged among themselves. Well before they were liberated during the Civil War, the black American community had already begun to organize itself with its own churches. Nonetheless, it was very difficult to achieve anything with no economic power and no resources at their disposal.

By the 1830s, the abolitionist (anti-slavery) movement in the North was well underway. These Northern Christians did not accept the rationalizations their Southern counterparts used to justify slavery. They saw slavery as barbaric and a violation of Christian teachings. They acquired a moral imperative to oppose it, sometimes willing to take personal risks and sacrifices for their cause.

To a great many others, however, it became more of an issue of economics and the balance of political power within the country. One must realize that, at that point in time, the permanent existence of the United States was by no means a certainty. The country was still regarded as an experiment in progress. It had not been around anywhere near as long as any of the other powerful nations of the world, and it was still possible that the South would break apart and go its separate way.

Many Americans, particularly those in the North, had come to believe that the country's best chance for survival as an independent democracy was to remain united. Presumably, there was strength in numbers. Furthermore, while the United States as a whole had a relatively well-balanced economy, individual sections were dangerously dependent on one economic sector or another. The South had agricultural products like tobacco and cotton for export, but it lacked the factories needed to make machinery for harvesting and transporting goods and to provide for the necessities of life. The North was not growing enough food and other agricultural products to be entirely self-sufficient, either. Urban poverty was more prominent in the North. The Southern states were, at that time, an important source of income and trade with the rest of the world. There was reason for each side to be uneasy about the prospect of being cut off from the other half of the nation.

In the decades preceding the Civil War, a series of compromises were made in U.S. Congress over the issue of slavery. The South was afraid that, as the country grew, eventually there would be more states in the North and the West than there were in the South. Since slavery wasn't as practical or desirable in these areas, there was reason to believe that, as the nation enlarged and added new states, the South would become increasingly isolated and outnumbered. If that occurred, it would be easy for the abolitionists to gain control of the Congress and to outlaw slavery across the entire nation, as so many Southerners feared.

The issue would come to a head whenever any of the new territories were ready to be admitted into the Union. One such crisis was resolved in the Missouri Compromise of 1820, which saw Maine (a free state) and Missouri (a slave state) simultaneously admitted to the Union. Other compromise bills tried to

$200 Reward.

RANAWAY from the subscriber, on the night of Thursday, the 30th of Sepember,

FIVE NEGRO SLAVES,

To-wit: one Negro man, his wife, and three children.

The man is a black negro, full height, very erect, his face a little thin. He is about forty years of age, and calls himself *Washington Reed*, and is known by the name of Washington. He is probably well dressed, possibly takes with him an ivory headed cane, and is of good address. Several of his teeth are gone.

Mary, his wife, is about thirty years of age, a bright mulatto woman, and quite stout and strong.

The oldest of the children is a boy, of the name of FIELDING, twelve years of age, a dark mulatto, with heavy eyelids. He probably wore a new cloth cap.

MATILDA, the second child, is a girl, six years of age, rather a dark mulatto, but a bright and smart looking child.

MALCOLM, the youngest, is a boy, four years old, a lighter mulatto than the last, and about equally as bright. He probably also wore a cloth cap. If examined, he will be found to have a swelling at the navel.

Washington and Mary have lived at or near St. Louis, with the subscriber, for about 15 years.

It is supposed that they are making their way to Chicago, and that a white man accompanies them, that they will travel chiefly at night, and most probably in a covered wagon.

A reward of $150 will be paid for their apprehension, so that I can get them, if taken within one hundred miles of St. Louis, and $200 if taken beyond that, and secured so that I can get them, and other reasonable additional charges, if delivered to the subscriber, or to THOMAS ALLEN, Esq., at St. Louis, Mo. The above negroes, for the last few years, have been in possession of Thomas Allen, Esq., of St. Louis.

WM. RUSSELL.

ST. LOUIS, Oct. 1, 1847.

Slaves who were able to escape were often rounded up and returned to their masters. Sometimes even free black men in the North were kidnapped and sold to Southern slaveowners.

maintain a balance in the number of slave states and free states. However, the system became increasingly complicated to manage. States that were capable of adopting an agricultural system like the Southern plantations wanted the option of going to a slavery system, since it was the only way they could compete agriculturally with the Southern states. In other states, however, it became clear that Southern-style plantations were not feasible for geographical or economic reasons. Consequently, there was less desire for slavery and it was easier to get the state to enter as a free state.

By the later stages of the 1850s, it became clear to some American politicians that the country was headed for disaster. Compromises were harder and harder to reach and there was a growing movement in the North for an out-and-out prohibition of slavery, if not in the

Portraits of Maj. Gen. Ulysses S. Grant, officer of the Federal Army (left)
and Gen. Robert E. Lee, officer of the Confederate Army (right).

entire country then at least in all new states that were being admitted.

In the election of 1860, those opposed to slavery, and the majority of Northerners (whether or not slavery was an important issue to them), sided with the new Republican Party. The Democrats were supported by an odd and uneasy coalition of Southerners and some Northerners who believed that it was necessary to continue compromising with the South in order to hold the country together. The Republicans put forth Abraham Lincoln as their candidate, the Democrats Stephen Douglas. Coincidentally, both men were from Illinois and had previously opposed one another in the earlier stages of their careers. Both men also held complex and somewhat changeable views on the issue of slavery.

Lincoln had wrestled with the topic in many ways over the years. At one time, he had been in favor of a colonization plan that would return the blacks to Africa, fearing that there was no way they could be freed and successfully assimilated into American society. Gradually, he began to side with the abolitionists. However, his primary concern seemed to be the preservation of the Union. He realized that the country could never be unified and strong as long as it remained divided over the slavery issue. Since it was not possible for the entire country to accept slavery, it seemed that, sooner or later, the only solution would be for the entire country to reject it.

Nonetheless, Lincoln did not initially push for the abolition of slavery, but rather for its containment within areas where it had traditionally existed. Douglas, on the other hand, while also not a great admirer of slavery, realized that much of his party's strength lay in the South. He seemed to believe that a continued pattern of compromise and negotiation with the South was the best way to hold the country together. He feared that the country would go to war if the Republican views were adopted. Ultimately, he was right.

Almost immediately after Abraham Lincoln's narrow election victory in 1860, the Southern states made plans to secede from the union, knowing full well that this would lead to a civil war. Lincoln's entire presidency was consumed with little else but waging this war. It began when Southern forces attacked a Union military base at Fort Sumter, South Carolina. Lincoln had been president for approximately six weeks when this event occurred. He would be assassinated by a conspiracy of angry and disgruntled Southerners led by John Wilkes Booth less than a week after the official end of the Civil War, when General Robert E. Lee of the South surrendered to General Ulysses S. Grant of the North at Appomattox Court House in Virginia, in April of 1865.

In the four long years between these events, more than 600,000 Americans would die as a direct result of the war, and some estimate the total casualties as high as 1 million. Many Americans today fail to grasp the significance of this harrowing statistic. There were more deaths during this war than in all other American-involved wars combined. In fact, during World War II, the number of Americans who died was slightly over 400,000.

This means that America lost considerably more men during the Civil War than it did in the war that is regarded as the world's most devastating conflict to date. Furthermore, America lost these men when its total population was a small fraction of what it was in 1940 (about 31 million at the time of the Civil War).

The four long years of the American Civil War are full of details about interesting military decisions, great victories, disgraceful defeats, and a great deal of confusion on both sides. At the start of the war, neither side was well equipped to fight. Ironically, most of the generals on both sides were former colleagues who were originally trained at West Point and became members of the United States Army. Some of them fought together against Mexico or against Native Americans. They knew each other well. However, because most Southerners felt more loyalty to their state than to the nation, some generals, like Robert E. Lee, who would become the leader of the Confederate Army, felt obliged to resign from the United States Army and take up corresponding positions among the rebel forces being mustered by their home states.

In many ways, the North seemed to have the decided advantage at the outset. They had the larger population and a long-established government and military system, with troops, weapons, forts, ships, and railroads already at hand. However, the United States had not been at war for several years and the military was ill-prepared, even in the North. While starting out with fewer resources, the South was able to use the fervor of Southern patriotism and the desire to have their own nation in order to inspire young men to join the military and assemble a fighting force with incredible speed.

Furthermore, history demonstrates that the South acquired superior military leaders in the break-up of the original U.S. Army. In the first couple of years of the war, the North suffered from incompetent commanders who were unable or unwilling to take decisive action to end the war. Lincoln was frequently frustrated with questionable decisions made on the battlefield, replacing the supreme commander of the Northern troops on several different occasions before finally promoting General Ulysses Grant to the position after the war had already dragged on for three years.

Although Lincoln had superior resources, he had to struggle against the fact that many Northerners did not feel extremely committed to fighting the war. While the South rallied around their cause, Northerners were frequently on the verge of giving up and turning to diplomatic efforts to try to find peace, even if it meant letting the Southern states go. Lincoln would not agree to do this. He devoted himself passionately, not only to waging the war but to convincing the people of the North of its importance. He saw it not only as an opportunity to put an end to slavery, but also as a means of preserving the Union and representative government.

When the very first scrimmage of the war took place at Bull Run, just outside Washington, D.C., a party of Northerners, Northern senators, gentlemen, and even some of their wives came down to watch, naively believing that the battle would be over quickly and that the Southern rebels would be routed.

They saw the entire event as a pleasant afternoon's amusement; some even brought along a picnic lunch. Even Lincoln himself assumed that the conflict could be ended quickly, since the initial call to arms for Northern recruits required an enlistment of only ninety days.

All too quickly, the country learned the horrible fate that awaited it. Not only were the Northern troops soundlybeaten at Bull Run and the spectators sent scurrying back to Washington, but this event was followed by defeat after defeat for the Union Army. While Southerners didn't really accomplish much by their victories, they nonetheless managed to buoy their spirits and convince the Southern people that their cause had a chance of success. The early victories were also enough to keep other nations from interfering in the conflict, since they could not presume that the North would be triumphant in the end and did not want to place themselves in a disadvantageous trade position with the South in the event that the rebels won.

The battle at Gettysburg, Pennsylvania, in 1863 represented the high point for the Southern forces in terms of their penetration into the North. Virtually all the rest of the major battles were fought on Southern territory. By 1864, it was clear that Southern forces were gradually being overwhelmed and driven from one area after another. The North put together a string of victories just in time to convince the people to stay with the campaign and allow Abraham Lincoln to be elected to a second term.

After the election of 1864, it quickly became clear that the end of the war was in

District of Columbia. Company E, 4th U.S. Colored Infantry, at Fort Lincoln.

sight and that the South would not prevail. By this point, the South's resources were seriously depleted. While the North suffered heavy losses, they were in a better position to continue the fight, and finally acquired some military leaders, notably Generals Grant and Sherman, who were able to outwit their Southern adversaries and mount successful campaigns. In the final months of the conflict, the South's losses were particularly devastating. Not only did the Union forces drive back the rebel troops, but they followed them into the South, destroying railroads, farmland and homes in an attempt to force the Confederacy and its president, Jefferson Davis, to surrender.

President Lincoln waited until well into the war to issue the Emancipation Proclamation, which began to free the slaves. The Proclamation itself is somewhat more complex than first meets the eye. Lincoln was actually reluctant to issue it for fear that it would further inflame the South and cause some neutral states along the border between both sides to join the Southern cause.

For this reason, it was only the first step toward full emancipation. The Proclamation technically freed only those slaves in rebel territory—places where the Union was not actually in control. Thus it was in many ways a

First reading of the Emancipation Proclamation before the cabinet.

symbolic act that signaled the Union's intention to gradually abolish slavery. Once the war finally ended, a series of constitutional amendments outlawed slavery once and for all.

Lincoln realized that, regardless of what he put on paper, his ability to free the slaves or do much of anything else required that he win the war militarily. Consequently, he did not wish to issue the Proclamation until he felt that it was a good military strategy. One eventual factor was the belief that the freed slaves would join the Northern forces and help overthrow their former masters. To a point, this happened, although there were also a smaller number of blacks who were pressed into the service of the South and forced to fight for the Confederate side as well.

Lincoln personally despised the institution of slavery and wished to abolish it, but his immediate goal was to preserve the Union. In order to do so, however, he had to summon the support of not only the abolitionists, but the border states that remained in the Union yet still permitted slavery. He was a practical politician who realized that, in order to accomplish any of his own objectives for the country, he had to enlist the cooperation of the majority of the American people. In fact, Lincoln was perhaps the first American president who was a skillful politician in the modern sense of the term. He was adept at motivating people, at focusing attention on issues and at getting ordinary people to respond to higher values.

At the time of his assassination, despite having had many previous detractors, he

Theodore Roosevelt and his "Rough Riders" became heroes for their exploits in the Battle of San Juan Hill.

became by far the most beloved figure in American history and already considered a great man internationally. People were grateful to him for more than winning the war and freeing the slaves. He had conferred upon the American people a sense of destiny and greatness. After the Civil War and after Lincoln, America was ready to be a powerful nation in the world for the first time.

However, the country took a few steps backwards before it was ready to move forward to enforce Lincoln's legacy. Due largely to anger over Lincoln's assassination, the presidents who immediately succeeded him took a hard line toward the reconstruction

of the South and against allowing it to participate fully once again in the national government. The South was financially ruined by the war, and Lincoln's successors became determined to keep it in a vulnerable position.

While the slaves were free on paper, the entire economy was in such ruins that, in many cases, the slaves had little alternative but to "voluntarily" go to work for their former masters in order to survive. White resentment towards the blacks for their role in toppling the Southern way of life led to an entrenchment of racial prejudice.

However, the economic ruination of the South was not entirely the product of the Civil

War. The world was gradually shifting away from agriculture-based economies towards the new industries of manufacturing and machinery. The South had been slow in developing these industries and was ill-positioned to make much progress after the war. As demand for cotton and other agricultural products waned or was filled in part by other producers, the South lost its economic base. Many parts of the South, both black and white, were plunged into a poverty from which, even to the present day, they have not completely emerged.

THE SPANISH-AMERICAN WAR

Spain was once one of the most powerful countries in the world, but by the mid-1890s it was barely hanging on to a handful of remaining colonies, after most of the rest had won independence. Cuba was a significant exception. Despite various attempts at rebellion, Spain still controlled this colony, one of its last thresholds in North America.

Because Cuba was located so close to Florida, for a long time there was a flourishing trade between the two. Consequently, Americans were readily sympathetic to the Cubans in their struggle for independence. The American zeal to support the revolutionary cause in Cuba was, however, fueled by some questionable journalistic tactics among various competing American newspapers, which blatantly exaggerated stories of Spanish atrocities in order to fan the public's interest and outrage over what was happening.

The U.S. president at the time was William McKinley. Initially, he worked hard to try to calm the situation and persuade Spain to abandon its harsh policies and come to peaceful terms with the Cubans. Unfortunately, again with some help from American newspapers, McKinley was portrayed as weak for not taking an aggressive stance.

The situation came to a head rather suddenly when a U.S. battleship, the USS Maine, exploded in Havana Harbor, killing most of its crew. Most historians today doubt very much that the Spanish had anything to do with this explosion. It may have been the work of Cuban rebels trying to provoke the U.S. to enter the war, or the mere result of an accidental coal fire. However, the American public seemed poised to believe that this was an act of unprovoked aggression by the Spanish, requiring a military response.

While Cuba was the site of the provocation between the United States and Spain, a significant part of this war was fought on the high seas and in and around Spain's last Pacific colonies, the Philippines and Guam. For various reasons, America was better prepared for naval warfare than for mounting a conquering army. Theodore Roosevelt, originally the assistant secretary of the Navy, went on to play a significant role in dispatching Commodore George Dewey to fight a decisive naval battle in Manila Bay in which many Spanish ships were destroyed. For a while thereafter, the American forces did relatively little, while Filipino rebels, analogous to the rebels in the Cuban colony, struggled against the Spanish fortresses on the islands.

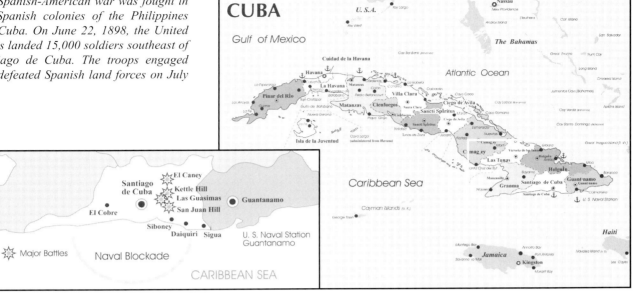

The Spanish-American war was fought in the Spanish colonies of the Philippines and Cuba. On June 22, 1898, the United States landed 15,000 soldiers southeast of Santiago de Cuba. The troops engaged and defeated Spanish land forces on July 1st.

From the start, Spain was in relatively poor shape to wage this sort of war and had little long-term hope of holding on to these disgruntled colonies. Despite the fact that there were blunders in the American military campaign, the Spanish surrendered in August of 1898 without really having put up much of a fight. Nonetheless, Americans, as they had been after the Mexican War, seemed pleased with another victory which further confirmed the country's sense of America's destiny and role as a leader of the free world.

If nothing else, America had a new hero, the likes of which it had not seen since the days of Abraham Lincoln and Ulysses S. Grant. He was Theodore Roosevelt, the former bureaucrat and assistant secretary from the Department of the Navy, who in the later

stages of the war had volunteered to become a colonel in the cavalry. He headed a unit known as the Rough Riders, made up of ranchers, businessmen, polo players and a few ex-convicts. Though the unit was intended to be a cavalry, after bungling an attempt to get their horses shipped from Tampa, they had to fight on foot. Nonetheless, they ended up playing a minor but dramatic role in the final military victory in the campaign, the Battle of San Juan Hill, in which the Spanish were soundly defeated, mainly because they made use of only 19,000 of the 200,000 soldiers that were available to them on the island of Cuba.

For various reasons, Cuba's independence had been guaranteed before the war had started, and so there was never any serious question of Cuba becoming part of the United

In spite of his initial reluctance, President William McKinley could not avoid bowing to political pressure. On April 11, 1898, he asked Congress for a declaration of war against Spain.

the twentieth century. We can discuss them here in the same section because there are remarkable similarities between the two. An often quoted expression, coined by Santayana and advanced by those who stress the importance of studying history, is "Those who fail to learn from history are doomed to repeat it." The world's involvement in these two major conflicts is probably one of the best cases in point to confirm the wisdom of such advice. The fact that the world learned relatively little from its experience with World War I doomed it to reenact the event some twenty years later.

The two conflicts are remarkably similar to one another in several ways, which also makes these wars very different than most that preceded them. Until this time, despite some minor alliances, wars were largely fought between two nations that had specific grievances with one another, or when one nation was trying to overthrow or occupy another. The World Wars represented the first significant time when many nations in the world took sides and joined into a broader and more complex conflict. While it is not quite true to say the entire world was embroiled in these wars, they did touch many different nations on several continents, either as direct participants or as settings for land, naval or aerial battles.

States, although it was a United States protectorate for a time. However, with the defeat of the Spanish, interest in the Philippines and Puerto Rico intensified. The Philippines would eventually become an independent nation, whereas Puerto Rico would become a U.S. territory. However, both events took several decades to be finally resolved.

THE WORLD WARS

Two world wars occupied much of American and global history in the first half of

The other point that distinguished these wars was the rapid escalation of warfare technology. For the first time, warplanes took to the skies and played a significant role in the outcome of battles. Bombs and artillery were much more sophisticated and devastating. Chemical weapons were used for the first time.

US 7th Machine Gun Battalion, 3rd Division at Chateau Thierry bridgehead (WWI).

Also, not for the first time in history, but atypical of the other conflicts in which America had been involved, there was greater willingness to target civilians. Commercial ships were deliberately destroyed. Residential sections of cities were systematically bombed. In short, war was no longer fought strictly between soldiers. It placed the lives of all citizens of the warring nations, and of those nations caught between, in serious jeopardy.

For this reason, these two wars were particularly devastating, and, when they were over, the nations of the world sincerely hoped and tried to believe that the lesson had finally been learned once and for all. After each of these wars, an attempt was made to join all of the nations of the world into an organization that would help provide peaceful means for resolving disputes and discourage countries from fighting one another. The organization formed after World War I, the League of Nations, was a failure. The United Nations, formed soon after World War II, was a qualified success and remains a significant presence in our world today. However, it has not been as successful in keeping our world free of armed conflicts as originally hoped.

Another interesting similarity between the two world wars is that America tried to stay out of both of them. They began between other nations in Europe and in Asia. We initially tried to remain neutral but, for one reason or another, were inevitably drawn into the conflicts. Once we did enter them, however, we took on a primary role in waging the struggles and pursuing them to ultimate victory, at a high cost to ourselves, both in lives and in dollars, especially the second time around.

The roots of the First World War are complex and, in many ways, startlingly petty. Over several years, various European nations took offense to the actions of their neighbors and began to form alliances. The balance of power was shifting in many ways, and the Industrial Revolution and the rapid growth of the arms race were significant factors. A former power, the Austro-Hungarian Empire, was declining. At the same time, under the leadership of the "Kaiser," Germany was expanding industrially and militarily in ways that alarmed some of its neighbors. There was animosity between Russia and Austria, and between France and Germany, as a result of past conflicts. Nonetheless, the event that triggered the start of the war, the assassination of Archduke Ferdinand of the Austro-Hungarian empire by an ethnic Serbian in 1914, hardly seemed, at the time, to deserve to be the start of one of the most bloody and devastating conflicts that the world had ever seen.

Before long, many European nations aligned themselves into one or the other of two camps. The one called the Central Powers included Germany, Austria-Hungary, Italy, Bulgaria and Turkey. The Allied Powers included England, France and Russia. Eventually, Italy would switch sides and join the Allied Powers as well.

In the beginning, Americans, like most of the world, did not believe that the conflict would become as serious or as lengthy as it did. The European nations had been squabbling and threatening one another for

quite some time, and there seemed little reason to take this latest round of scrimmages seriously. Even among those who did fear the worst, many staunchly believed that this was a European matter and that it was vitally important for America to stay out of it. After all, so many different nations were involved, and we had relationships of one kind or another with countries on both sides.

Gradually, however, American sympathies began to drift decidedly towards the Allies. To begin with, England was still regarded as an ancestral homeland and a sister nation by many Americans. Americans were also sympathetic towards the French, against whom America had never been at war, and who had modeled its own democratic republic to some extent upon the American one. There were also a great many German Americans who became distressed at any suggestion of joining the

EUROPE
Before and After World War I

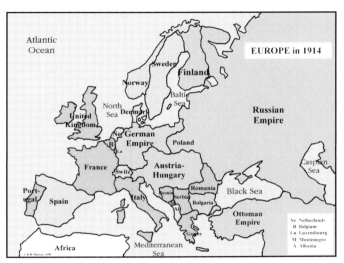

Allied cause. They joined with Irish Americans in vigorously promoting the cause of American neutrality. Furthermore, there was animosity against the Russians, particularly by many Jews who traced their lineage to Russia and Poland, and since the Russians and the Germans were at odds, this seemed to provoke some sympathy towards Germany.

During the first two years of the conflict in Europe, Americans participated in many efforts aimed at negotiating an end to the fighting. However, neutrality proved to be a difficult stance to keep. For one, a significant amount of the war was fought on the seas. The naval battles, involving warships and, for the first time, submarines, posed a threat to the ships of neutral nations. Also, Americans were placed at risk when they traveled on commercial vessels that belonged to one of the warring countries, since not only warships but commercial vessels as well became targets as the conflict escalated. American interests also suffered from blockades which were established by one nation outside another nation's ports.

When the Germans sank the English luxury liner the Lusitania in 1915, it was a provocation that significantly tipped the balance of American public opinion towards the Allied cause. Although Americans died on the Lusitania, it is also true that the Germans had warned Americans against traveling on the

Woodrow Wilson's firm belief that the seas should be kept safe from German U-boats, coupled with growing pro-British sentiments in the United States led to America entering World War I on April 6, 1917.

Lusitania and that the ship, was carrying, in addition to passengers, small arms and explosives that had been purchased in the United States.

Nonetheless, both the Germans and American President Woodrow Wilson still wanted to keep the United States out of the conflict. Indeed, Wilson won his re-election in 1916 on a platform which featured the slogan, "He kept us out of war."

The reasons America finally did go to war are complex and are still open to some dispute among historians. However, there is general consensus that a significant factor was the escalation of the German war effort against England and the risk that England would lose the war unless America joined. Clearly, American business interests favored a British

victory. As well, Americans were outraged when Germany attempted to persuade Mexico to enter into an alliance and attack the U.S.

Once it became clear to the Germans that the Americans were likely to enter the war, they launched an all-out naval attack in an attempt to starve Britain into submission before Americans could launch their own troops into battle.

By the time America entered the war in 1917, things were already going poorly for the Allies. The British and French were unable to advance the trench lines against Germany. The Russians were weak due to heavy casualties and an internal revolution that would soon knock them out of the war and allow Germany to shift all its troops to the western front. (Russia would shortly thereafter turn into a communist dictatorship known as the Soviet Union.)

It is beyond question that American soldiers arrived in Europe just in time to break the stalemate and tip the scales in favor of the Allies. Most specifically, our troops were instrumental in enabling the British and French to defeat the Germans. The fighting on the border between France and Germany had become so devastating that large parts of the countryside were transformed into wastelands denuded of vegetation by continuous shelling and the digging of foxholes and fortifications. Once it became clear to the Germans that they had lost their military advantage, they surrendered on November 11, 1918.

Of the 58 million soldiers who had participated in World War I, less than 5 million were Americans. Of the 8 million or more people who had been killed, only 112,000 were Americans. Nonetheless, America played a decisive role in the Allied victory, and our contribution was greatly appreciated by the French and British in particular. Both of these countries were badly maimed in the conflict, and Germany and Russia had been soundly defeated. Thus, the United States was the only country in a position to celebrate the final outcome, since the price we had paid for victory was comparatively light.

Following World War I, Germany was in no condition to mount any sort of military presence. The allies made sure, through the terms of surrender worked out in the Versailles Treaty, that Germany was punished for allegedly instigating the conflict and that it would not be able to pose a threat in the near future.

In the meantime, the well-to-do elements of the Western world soon entered a period of great, almost reckless prosperity in the 1920s, followed by the severe, worldwide Great Depression of the 1930s. For a time, thoughts of international power struggles were replaced by economic concerns and a preoccupation with domestic issues. Thus, the world lost its attentiveness and failed to appreciate what was happening in Germany and Japan, as well as Italy, until it was too late to head off the dire consequences.

The League of Nations was a concept Woodrow Wilson fought hard to establish as a means of protecting the world from future devastating confrontations. However, it failed, mainly because, despite Wilson's efforts, the United States, for various internal political reasons, refused to participate in it.

In the meantime, the punishments and sanctions placed upon Germany devastated and humiliated the German people and greatly contributed to their willingness to follow Adolf Hitler, whose highly nationalistic and racist policies aimed at overcoming the oppressive foreign control of Germany and reestablishing it as a world power. Meanwhile, the growth of the Japanese empire under Emperor Hirohito was all but ignored by much of the Western world, since the nations immediately menaced, such as China, were far away and relatively unimportant in light of the economic crisis at home.

World War II played out much like World War I, except that American involvement lasted for a considerably longer period of time and took a far heavier toll in casualties. In World War II, Germany, Italy and Japan aligned themselves against much of the rest of the world, primarily the United States, Great Britain, France, Russia, and China. By then, Russia was firmly entrenched in communist dictatorship and was not overly friendly with any of the other Allied nations. However, Russia was more or less forced into the Allied camp when it was attacked by Germany.

Once again, although American sympathies leaned heavily toward the Allied nations, there were substantial sentiments to keep out of the conflict. The country was working to try to emerge from ten years of depression and economic misery, and the military was unprepared for another war.

However, on December 7, 1941, the Japanese attacked a U.S. naval base at Pearl Harbor in Hawaii. The attack caught America

The Big Three — Stalin, Roosevelt, and Churchill —
during a peace conference in 1943.

by surprise and inflicted devastating casualties, both to servicemen and to ships. Shortly thereafter, the United States declared war against both Japan and Germany and began to mobilize for the most complex military campaign has ever launched.

During the four long years of American involvement in the war, a great many significant events occurred. As in World War I, for a time things went badly for the Allied forces, as both the Germans and the Japanese occupied more and more conquered territory. They were finally repelled on both fronts, and once again the American military and industrial involvement was critical in turning the tide. The Germans were eventually defeated by the combined Allied forces, which simultaneously

drove them back on all sides. The Russians advanced from the east, and the Americans and British from the west. For four years, France was occupied by the Germans and its interim government cooperated with the Nazis. Thus, France was taken out of the conflict, so once again that nation needed to be liberated by the Americans and British, on their way towards driving the Germans back and ultimately surrounding and defeating them. With both the Russians and the Americans poised to enter Berlin, Hitler committed suicide in April of 1945, shortly before the final defeat and surrender of his forces.

This did not spell an end to the global conflict, however, as the Japanese still needed to be defeated. Although American forces had begun to

Dwight Eisenhower giving orders to American paratroopers in England

turn the tide in the Pacific as well, it still appeared that the ultimate defeat of the Japanese would still be some time away. However, throughout the course of the war, the United States and Germany had been engaged in a race to develop atomic weapons. The United States won the race, and on August 6 and 9, 1945, President Harry Truman authorized the dropping of two atomic bombs on the Japanese cities of Hiroshima and Nagasaki.

Days later, the Japanese surrendered and the entire conflict finally came to a halt. By that time, over 400,000 Americans had been killed or died as a result of the war. Europe was once again devastated by bombs and artillery. Furthermore, the world would soon learn of the atrocities committed by the Nazi Germans, including the extermination of approximately 6 million Jews. While Americans once again celebrated victory, this time the price was so high that it was not achieved without heavy hearts and ongoing anxieties for the future.

KOREA AND VIETNAM

After having sat back too long watching Nazi Germany, the Soviet Union, and Communist China develop into dangerous military powers, America became determined to act quickly to head off the early signs of communist infiltration into other parts of the world. After World War II, the United States entered into alliances with many other democratic nations, particularly those in

Europe and Asia, and with Canada, Australia, and New Zealand, to help protect against the threat of a communist invasion. These alliances were swiftly put to the test, first in Korea, then later in Vietnam.

Although the Soviet Union (also known as the U.S.S.R.) had been America's ally in World War II, political and ideological differences caused significant tension between the two superpowers after the war. The Soviet Union imposed communism on many Eastern European countries, such as Poland, East Germany, and Czechoslovakia, and it encouraged communist revolutions in China and North Korea. The U.S. was staunchly opposed to the spread of communism, but it was fully aware that a war against a country as vast and as powerful as the Soviet Union would be devastating. Instead, the U.S. and the Soviet Union would for the next forty-five years or so engage in a geopolitical standoff known as the Cold War. Although the two superpowers never officially went to war against one another, their opposition led the U.S. to use its military power to prevent the spread of communism into other countries such as Korea and Vietnam.

There are many similarities, both superficial and significant, between the Korean War and the Vietnam War. In light of this, it is suitable to analyze them in the same chapter. Both countries were divided in two, with a communist government to the north and a non-communist government to the south. The United States stepped in as an ally to the government in the south in order to protect them from being overrun by communists who were determined to unify the country under a single communist regime. Both wars required

American troops to fight on foreign soil and in parts of the world with which they had little previous experience or familiarity. The terrain was largely woodland, tundra or jungle, which worked to the advantage of our enemies, who were familiar with these elements and could use them to conceal their operations.

A further complication lay in the fact that both our friends and foes were of the same race and nationality, and spoke the same language. It was often difficult to tell them apart, and this made it difficult to know if "friendly" villages were being infiltrated by agents working for the other side. Particularly in Vietnam, we fought not only against the North Vietnamese, but also against Viet Cong rebels within South Vietnam who were sympathetic to the communist cause. Many of these rebels were civilians who would sometimes recruit peasants, women, and even children to carry out acts of sabotage or terrorism in an attempt to unnerve American troops, confuse them, and diminish their will to fight. It was easy for communist politicians to portray us as the foreigners and aggressors, the ones who shouldn't be there.

Ultimately, especially in Vietnam, it was easy for many Americans back home to believe that we actually were invaders. There was increasing frustration with or opposition to these conflicts among the American public, particularly when they dragged on. Victory seemed doubtful, despite the high financial cost and the number of lives lost.

The Korean War began under the presidency of Harry Truman, following a North Korean attack on June 25, 1950.

President Harry Truman

General Douglas MacArthur was put in command of American troops sent, with the blessing of the United Nations, to conduct a "police action" to prevent the North Koreans from attacking and overrunning their neighbors to the south.

Initially, MacArthur's first strike against the North was so successful that it appeared the conflict would immediately end in victory. However, the Chinese, under Communist Party Chairman Mao Zedong, sent troops to support the North Koreans, who repelled the Americans back beyond the boundary line between the North and the South. There, a difficult and bloody guerilla war was conducted for approximately two years with troops advancing from hill to hill and capturing or giving up small pieces of territory in endless scrimmages that settled very little. With the Chinese drawn into the struggle, America's worst fears about the spread of communism and the danger posed by Communist China seemed to become reality, and the long-term cost of surrender seemed far too risky.

The American people were clearly frustrated. Less than five years since the end of World War II, there was suddenly a large force of young Americans again sent into battle, of whom 54,000 would die and many more would be wounded. Armistice talks were scheduled frequently between the two sides, but produced little in the way of results. In many ways, the Chinese were more content with the stalemate than the Americans, and thus had little incentive to end the fighting.

Many Americans, particularly those in the military, feared that all-out war with mainland China might become inevitable (and some wanted it to happen). Indeed, there was soon much at stake in this situation that had begun as a "police action."

The situation deteriorated when General Douglas MacArthur publicly criticized President Truman, accusing him of being responsible for preventing MacArthur from bombing supply depots in Manchuria, which MacArthur thought would lead to victory. This unprecedented attack on Truman, the commander-in-chief, caused division within the military and forced Truman to fire MacArthur. Because MacArthur had also been a hero during the Second World War, this only further divided the American public, the right-wing of whom cheered MacArthur and were critical of Truman.

As the war dragged on, America became suspicious and disillusioned at home. The euphoria of the decisive military victory and the end of World War II had been spoiled by the growing menace of the Soviet Union in Europe and the inability to drive back the Communist Chinese in Korea. Many people became paranoid about communism and feared that communist sympathizers at home were partly responsible for the failures abroad. This led to a "witch-hunt," led by Senator Joseph McCarthy, in which Americans were investigated and often forced to sign loyalty oaths attesting they had no allegiance to the Communist Party.

All these events at home led to a change in government. In the election of 1952, another

The popular General Douglas MacArthur served the nation in World War I as a major (and later brigadier general), in World War II as commander of the army in the Far East, and in the Korean War as head of the United Nations military forces.

war hero, former General Dwight D. Eisenhower, became a Republican president. Eisenhower campaigned, in part, on a promise to end the conflict in Korea, and it was a promise he fulfilled soon after taking office. Partly because he implicitly threatened to use the atomic bomb to end the stalemate, Eisenhower managed to convince the Chinese and North Koreans to end the hostilities on July 26, 1953. The peace agreement left North and South Korea as separate nations and set up a demilitarized zone between the two. To this day, North Korea remains a communist nation and South Korea a democracy and an American ally (with an ongoing American military presence).

Did America win the war in Korea? If the objective was to halt the spread of communism into South Korea, the answer is yes. However, America clearly paid a price for its victory, not only in dollars and in lives, but also in division and disagreement at home about our role as a policeman to the world. Most Americans were satisfied with the victory and looked forward to the return of a more normal life under the strength and stability of President Eisenhower. However, the great communist menace was still out there and had proven its tenacity and willingness to fight, at any cost, for its cause. Few Americans had reason to believe that another conflict would be too distant on the horizon.

Soon after, America would learn the hard way that what had been difficult to achieve in Korea would prove impossible to achieve in Vietnam. The Vietnam War was a longer and more devastating military conflict than the war in Korea, and one which clearly did not end the way America would have liked it to. We suffered a high number of casualties (58,000 dead) and, in addition to the lives lost on the battlefield, we watched our nation be torn apart with angry disagreement about the war, which often erupted into violent demonstrations. Henry Kissinger, the National Security Advisor under President Nixon, worked to negotiate a peaceful end to the war and has since conceded that some mistakes were made by American military and political leaders. However, he feels that a significant amount of blame for the loss in Vietnam lies with the American civilian protestors at home who effectively restricted the political power of the administration to act, and propelled it to seek a negotiated peace settlement which had little hope of holding up for very long. Opponents of Kissinger's

viewpoint argue that the war in Vietnam could never be won without unacceptable and possibly catastrophic risks of provoking another world war, and that American leadership should have recognized this and pulled back many years before it did.

To this day, Americans have strong opinions on the Vietnam War and are seriously divided over how history should view the war and America's role in it. On one hand, it is possible to make a case for the fact that America was engaged on foreign soil where it had no business being, fighting an enemy it did not understand with relatively little support from the people it was trying to defend, and with methods that produced incredible destruction and loss of life, not only among soldiers but also a great many civilians. On the other hand, many politicians and citizens felt that America's military involvement in Korea and Vietnam was necessary and justified to contain communism. One explanation that President Eisenhower (and others after him) gave for America's intervention was the "domino theory": if one nation succumbed to a communist revolution, its neighboring countries might also fall, like dominos, to the communist influence. There seemed to be little reason to hope that either the Soviet Union or China would ever back down in their efforts to oppose the United States and to spread their communist ideology over large portions of the world. Thus it was deemed necessary to America's interests that action be taken, even in places like Vietnam that posed no direct threat to American security.

However you may personally feel about the matter, there can be little doubt that the results

Television played a critical role in forming popular opinion as, for the first time, disturbing images of death and destruction were broadcast to Americans on a nightly basis via the evening news (left). Lyndon Johnson's efforts to escalate America's involvement in the conflict were not well received at home, particularly among younger voters (right).

of the American war effort in Vietnam were unsuccessful and unfortunate. The war began, much as it had in Korea, as a "police action," in which a limited number of American military experts were supposed to act in an advisory capacity to help the South Vietnamese improve their own military capabilities in order to resist the threat from the Communist North. Eventually, the entire Johnson and Nixon presidencies would be consumed in a frustrating effort to defeat communist forces and sympathizers who simply would not give up.

From the Communists' point of view, they were defending their homeland from foreign infiltrators. Though they suffered even heavier casualties than the Americans, it was a price they seemed willing to pay. They recruited boys in their early teens, put rifles into their hands, and sent them into the jungles to fight. The North Vietnamese were willing to suffer enormously for victory.

The details of the many years of fighting in Vietnam (which actually began with the French, since Vietnam had been a French colony) are interesting, but too extensive to be dealt with adequately here. The American war effort on behalf of the South Vietnamese involved land battles, some naval battles, and extensive air strikes. As the conflict escalated, more and more troops were sent to Vietnam. Eventually, especially under the presidency of Richard Nixon, devastating bombing campaigns were launched against North Vietnam, and eventually Cambodia, in an attempt to cripple the North Vietnamese forces which were once again being supplied and supported by the Communist Chinese.

One difference this time was that the United States did not dare pose the threat of a nuclear war, for it was by now clear to all Americans that, with the nuclear capabilities of the Soviet Union and Communist China, such a conflict could result in the extermination of much of the human race. The American military was placed in the frustrating position of always having limits on how far they could go and what they could do in order to impose their superior military technology upon the enemy.

Despite these limits, devastating acts of destruction were carried out by American troops. The technology of warfare had escalated rapidly, even since the relatively high-tech operation of World War II. In Vietnam, powerful new weapons were introduced. A chemical called napalm was dropped by bombers onto the jungle, instantly setting it afire, killing or maiming many soldiers and civilians trapped in the area and causing obliteration of the landscape. Once again, American troops were fighting in a situation where it was difficult to tell the allies from the enemies. Civilian women and children were sometimes strapped with bombs or feigned begging for help in an attempt to lure American troops into ambushes. Sometimes, American military leaders in the field made devastating and unconscionable mistakes in judgment in dealing with these situations. The My Lai massacre caught world-wide attention when American troops rounded up and executed many civilians in a village sympathetic to the enemy.

More than in any other previous war, the Vietnam War was fought not only on the battlefield, but also on American television screens. An unprecedented number of photo journalists followed the American forces and captured many terrifying scenes on film. Americans got used to seeing killing and devastation every night on the news. Statistics about American and enemy casualties were announced like baseball scores. There were harrowing scenes of civilians being summarily executed by South Vietnamese police officers and naked villagers running screaming from their destroyed homes, their bodies covered in napalm burns and shrapnel wounds. Americans saw their soldiers being loaded onto stretchers, bloody, with parts of limbs blown off by mines, booby traps, or enemy fire.

Month after month, year after year, America was no closer to a military victory. Instead, increasing numbers of young Americans received draft notices and were pressed into military service. Opposition to the war mounted, and the U.S. became increasingly polarized over the issue.

Richard Nixon was elected president in 1968 in part on the promise of finding "peace with honor" in Vietnam. He convinced the public that he could find a way to end the fighting without having to surrender and have the American sacrifice be in vain. To some, it appeared that he had been successful when the Paris Peace Accord ended the fighting on January 26, 1973. However, the accord required that America pull its combat troops out of Vietnam within sixty days, even through the South Vietnamese were still in no position to defend their borders without us. Over the next two years, the conflict continued to simmer. Then, in April 1975, the North Vietnamese army launched a devastating campaign into the south. It resulted in the absolute defeat of the South Vietnamese, the capture of Saigon, and the reunification of North and South Vietnam under one communist government. After having spent $150 billion and seeing over 58,000 Americans killed and a great many more wounded, America watched everything it had fought for go down the drain.

It would be a bitter pill for the American people to swallow and it would radically affect our thinking and willingness to engage in military conflicts on foreign soil. Although we have participated in other conflicts under the auspices of the United Nations or NATO (most notably the Gulf War against Iraq and the conflict in Yugoslavia), since Vietnam, America has been reluctant to commit itself to the type of lengthy, full-scale war effort it fought in Korea and Vietnam. The reluctance is often called the "Vietnam syndrome."

1. Name at least one of the Civil War battles that was fought on Northern (Union) soil.

2. The Stamp Act was one of many irritants that led to which American war?

3. Which American general (and later president) defeated the British in the Battle of New Orleans in 1815?

4. Which state was once an independent nation known as the Lone Star Republic?

5. Who assassinated President Lincoln shortly after the end of the Civil War?

6. Who was president of the United States when America entered World War I?

7. Who was president of the United States when America dropped two atomic bombs on Japan, an act which led directly to the end of World War II?

8. The fighting that would lead to the Vietnam War originally started when Vietnam was a colony of which European nation?

★ ★ ★ ★ ★ ★ ★ ★ ★ ★ ★

ANSWERS TO QUIZ TWO

1- Gettysburg, Antietam   2- Revolutionary War   3- Andrew Jackson

4- Texas   5- John Wilkes Booth   6- Woodrow Wilson

7- Harry Truman   8- France

OUR GREATEST
Presidents and Leaders

Several of our
nation's leaders are
remembered for the
manner in which they
rose to the challenges of
the day with courage,
skill, and vigor.

MOUNT RUSHMORE NATIONAL MEMORIAL

Mount Rushmore National Memorial, located in southwestern South Dakota, features the heads of United States presidents George Washington, Thomas Jefferson, Theodore Roosevelt, and Abraham Lincoln carved into a granite bluff. The massive sculpture was carved into the rim of Mount Rushmore 500 feet above the valley floor. Each head is about 60 feet tall.

We hold these truths to be sacred and undeniable;
that all men are created equal and independent,
that from that equal creation they derive rights inherent and inalienable,
among which are the preservation of life, and liberty, and the pursuit of happiness.

excerpt from the Declaration of Independence
THOMAS JEFFERSON
1743-1826

A man who is good enough to shed his blood for the country
is good enough to be given a square deal afterwards.
More than that, no man is entitled to, and less than that no man shall have.

THEODORE ROOSEVELT
1858-1919

And so, my fellow Americans:
ask not what your country can do for you - ask what you can do for your country.

JOHN FITZGERALD KENNEDY
1917-1963

THE CONCEPT OF GREATNESS

There have been countless Americans, in both public and private life, who have made a significant and lasting impact not only upon our nation, but also upon the development of the modern world. We will select, from the many, a handful of models that can be used to help us better understand the American character and the way in which great Americans have been produced by our country and impelled toward notable achievements.

The concept of greatness is particularly relevant in the study of American history because, particularly since the late 1800s, we have perceived ourselves as a great nation and have striven to occupy a leadership role in the world. Our form of government has served as a model for many of the world's modern democracies. We were instrumental in preserving the free world through the devastation of the two world wars. Many of the great scientific and medical breakthroughs of the twentieth century were the products of American individuals and institutions. We were the first nation to put a man on the moon and to land an unmanned spacecraft on Mars. We have pioneered such inventions as the automobile, the television and the computer, which have revolutionized modern life around the world. We have discovered the cures for

JOHN F. KENNEDY
1917-1963

Although he only served three years of his term in office before his assassination, President John Fitzgerald Kennedy remains one of the most popular leaders of the twentieth century. His legacy includes a host of accomplishments, such as the creation of the space program and important civil rights legislation.

perfect society, but we are a society that sets very high standards for our citizens and our leaders.

Greatness is of course a subjective concept. Over and above how other nations see us, even in looking at ourselves we often disagree as to which American leaders were "great."

Historically, we have come to regard several presidents from the 1700s and 1800s as particularly great men. Some historians complain that we look back upon them with "rose-colored glasses," remembering only their successes and their strong points and minimizing their personal and political failures. Furthermore, there seems to be a tendency not to take our present-day leaders quite as seriously as our leaders of old.

While most Americans consider George Washington and Abraham Lincoln to be great men, you would be hard-pressed to get agreement to assigning the quality of "greatness" to any of our post-World War II presidents. It is useful to ponder the reason for this. Is it that we are producing inferior leaders today, or is it simply that our concept of greatness and our willingness to accept "heroes" has changed as our society has

numerous diseases and have played an important role in the development of Western medicine. Our military continues to be technologically superior to any other in the world.

None of this is to say that America does not have problems. In many parts of the world, we are perceived as a violent country, a place that imposes our will upon other nations and suffers from extremes of wealth and poverty and social injustice and racial intolerance at home. Although we have worked hard to correct these problems and have learned from some of our mistakes, the accusations are nonetheless valid. We are not a greatness to a degree that many historians have come to assign it, whether or not it has been fully deserved. We will also look at those presidents who were pivotal in making significant changes to our country.

We have come a long way since the Declaration of Independence, and that tremendous growth and change has not always been a gradual and steady process. There were dramatic spurts during the administrations of particular presidents when we became a very different society from what we had been previously. In that sense, the greatness of the leaders of those times can be measured by the influence they had on our culture and political system.

GEORGE WASHINGTON

George Washington, America's first president, grew up in Virginia and began working as a surveyor of the land in his native colony. He rose to the rank of brigadier general during the French and Indian War of 1754 to 1763, in which Britain solidified its hold on colonial North America. Washington then began a political career when he was elected to the House of Burgesses, the legislative assembly of colonial Virginia. He was later elected to the first and second Continental Congresses, the colonial bodies that led to the Declaration of Independence and the eventual formation of the first truly American government.

George Washington
1732-1799

matured both intellectually and politically? Is it that we look too closely at our current leaders and see their blemishes and faults, whereas those of leaders in bygone eras were better hidden? Or is it simply a question of ideology? For many Democrats, John Kennedy and Bill Clinton deserve to be added to the ranks of great American presidents. To Republicans, Ronald Reagan surely belongs among their number.

In this section, we will not enter into political disputes by favoring those presidents of one party or another. Rather, we will assign

Washington's life serves to demonstrate that men are not always born into greatness. Sometimes the role is thrust upon them in a particular situation where they find themselves poised to influence the outcome of a significant historical event. Between 1775 and his death in 1799, George Washington would participate in nearly all the significant activities that gave birth to our nation. He did so not without difficulties and occasional setbacks, but he achieved much ultimate success. Without him, it is questionable whether our nation would ever have been born, or whether it would have made a firm enough start to survive.

Washington became the commander of the colonial forces in June 1775 and was instrumental in driving the British from Boston in March 1776. His victories undoubtedly helped inspire the colonials to their bold move of declaring independence in July 1776, giving them the will to persevere through the six long and difficult years of the Revolutionary War. Although, at times, Washington's army suffered greatly and tottered on the edge of defeat, he ultimately prevailed and helped force the surrender of British General Cornwallis in Yorktown, Virginia in 1781.

The defeat of the British cleared the way for the establishment of the first true American system of government, and Washington was chosen to be the president of the Constitutional Convention in 1787. This led to the first presidential election in 1789. Washington was elected our first president, and reelected in 1792. During the many years of his presidency, he helped solidify our form of government and established a precedent for the role of the presidency, from which it has not significantly departed.

George Washington was our first great leader and president, and he would also set the mold for some of the traits we look for in other American leaders. To begin with, although he was not born poor, Washington certainly had qualities as a hard-working, self-made man. Washington proved himself to be brave in the face of battle and firm in defending America. He also allowed his life to become consumed with service to the nation. Although he was a slaveholder, he made arrangements for the emancipation of his slaves after his wife's death.

It cannot be stressed enough how vulnerable the new nation was at the time Washington led it. Quite possibly, under someone of less dedication and determination, it may have proved to be an experiment doomed to failure.

Benjamin Franklin
1706-1790

BENJAMIN FRANKLIN

Another person who was instrumental in the founding of the United States was Benjamin Franklin, a political leader and statesman who also made numerous other contributions to American culture beyond the realm of politics. Franklin was remarkable for his incredible energy and the diversity of his lifetime achievements in a broad range of fields, including printing and publishing, writing, science, inventions, and diplomacy. He was born in Boston and moved to Philadelphia. He was the tenth of seventeen children and grew up with relatively little formal education but a lot of hard work, resourcefulness, and resiliency. He began working for his brother in a print shop at the age of twelve and grew into that trade, eventually publishing the Pennsylvania Gazette, a colonial newspaper, and Poor Richard's Almanac, a book of proverbs and personal advice which became popular in its time. He lived much of his adult life in the colony of Pennsylvania, and was instrumental in public service there, helping establish a fire department, a library, and a university. His autobiography endures as a significant literary work.

Remarkably, in the early 1750s, Franklin shifted his area of interest from the arts to the sciences. He became wealthy through various business ventures related to science and electricity. He is credited with the invention of the Franklin stove, bifocal spectacles, and the lightning rod, among other inventions.

For a time, he lived and worked in London, where he was a diplomatic representative for the colonies. As the Revolutionary War began to seem like an inevitability, he returned to Pennsylvania and began to play an active role in the drive for independence. He was a delegate to the second Continental Congress and helped draft the Declaration of Independence. During the war, he sought military and financial aid from France and became enormously popular with the French people. He was instrumental in helping to negotiate peace with Great Britain at the end of the war and worked on adoption of the U.S. Constitution.

Franklin, like Washington, helped to define the American character and the traits we

Franklin also serves as a model for the best in American diplomacy. He possessed a persistent friendliness and amicability which helped persuade other world leaders. While Washington was essential to the military success of the revolution, Franklin was critical to fostering a diplomatic climate which would enable Washington to continue his efforts and eventually persevere. Though Franklin was never president, his contributions to the development of American government and culture were extraordinary.

ABRAHAM LINCOLN

In the eyes of many historians, Abraham Lincoln is the greatest of all American heroes. This is somewhat ironic, as a close look at Lincoln's life shows a great deal of suffering and a long, hard struggle in which there were at least as many defeats as victories. Still, the personality of Lincoln emerges as a powerful force in defining the very best of American principles and values. Respected the world over, Lincoln came to stand for honesty, integrity, wisdom, dedication and perseverance.

Lincoln was born into extreme poverty in Kentucky in 1809. With but the sweat of his own brow, he managed to acquire a self-taught education which eventually enabled him to serve as a lawyer in Illinois in the 1830s and '40s. His diligent study of American history and the philosophies of former American and world leaders inspired him to seek a political life. He served one term in the House of

Abraham Lincoln
1809-1865

consider praiseworthy and commendable. The first was that Franklin pulled himself out of poverty to achieve both financial and political success. This has become a great part of the "American dream," the belief that, for those with courage, resourcefulness, and creativity, there are few limits to possible achievements within our nation. He is admired for his sense of humor and his wit, but also for his courage. It must be realized that, at the time the Declaration of Independence was signed, the signers, including Franklin, had reason to fear that if the Revolutionary War went badly for the colonists, the signers could be hanged as traitors.

Md. Allan Pinkerton, President Lincoln, and Major Gen. John A. McClernand, Antietam, October 3rd, 1862.

Representatives between 1847 and 1849. In 1856, he became a member of the new Republican Party, which was formed to stop the expansion of slavery.

The extraordinary transformation that would occur in his life over the next four years is virtually unique in American history. In 1858, he lost in a campaign to win the United States Senate seat of Stephen Douglas. Despite his defeat, he engaged in a series of well-documented debates with Douglas that remain important pieces of American political literature. They helped gain him national attention with his views against slavery, and in favor of democracy and civic duty. Nonetheless, it could hardly have been imagined by anyone, least of all Lincoln himself, that two years later he would be

elected president and that, almost immediately thereafter, the remainder of his life would become dedicated to the bloodiest and most crucial of all American wars.

By the time he was elected president in 1860, the country was already firmly headed down the road to Civil War. Indeed, the Southern states began the action to secede from the Union between the time Lincoln was elected and when he took office. Lincoln had little choice but either to sit back and watch the country be split in two, and quite possibly be destroyed as a result, or to wage a war for which the nation was largely unprepared.

He chose the latter route, and, for four long years, managed to maintain enough public support for an increasingly costly military campaign despite many vehement critics. The

President Lincoln's box at Ford's Theater, Washington, D.C.

two issues at stake were the abolition of slavery and the preservation of the Union, the latter of which was especially important to Lincoln. He gave stirring speeches, urging Americans to appreciate their freedom and to fight to keep America a strong nation where their representative government and free way of life could endure. At that time, democracy was still a limited experiment and its ultimate success was by no means assured. The Civil War questioned the very concept of whether any large nation could hold itself together through compromise among democratically elected representatives drawn together from all its different regions and subcultures.

Lincoln issued the Emancipation Proclamation to take effect on January 1, 1863. The Proclamation freed slaves only in areas of rebellion—not in the border states that were still part of the Union. As previously mentioned, his delay in issuing the proclamation was largely fueled by military strategy. In the first years of the war, Lincoln faced numerous frustrations, due largely to inexperience and incompetence on the part of many of his generals. For a while, victory seemed by no means assured and public support for the conflict began to falter. Lincoln delayed declaring freedom for the slaves until he felt that he was in a position to enforce his edict with a military victory that would make it more than just a document. The Union's victory at Antietam eventually served purpose for him.

Abraham Lincoln was assassinated by John Wilkes Booth at Ford's Theater on April 14, 1865, just a few days after the surrender of the Confederate forces formalized the Union victory. There is no doubt that Lincoln's assassination helped to cement his place in history. However, it would be unfair to suggest that this event had anything to do with his worthiness for admiration as a great American leader. Even before he actually gave his life in a literal sense, Lincoln had given himself over physically, mentally, and emotionally to the nation. It is startling to see the photographic record of the change in Lincoln's appearance from the date of his first election to the final days of the war. Clearly, the long hours of anxiety and determined effort took a toll upon him. His life was also marked by personal tragedy: the death of two sons at young ages, a stressful marriage, bouts of depression, and a lack of self-confidence. Lincoln certainly did

Theodore Roosevelt
1858-1919

not foresee the large number of lives that would be lost before the Civil War could be won, and the deaths weighed heavily upon his conscience throughout his administration.

Abraham Lincoln forever changed the image of the American hero. The country saw in him a model of self-sacrifice, a steady hand and a level head to guide the country through difficult times and maintain its sense of purpose and resolve to succeed. Like many other heroes, he was a self-made man who rose from humble beginnings. He was also clearly an intelligent man who left behind a great body of writing that has influenced

many other American presidents and world leaders to this day. He helped us to redefine ourselves as a nation, and managed to preserve the Union and abolish slavery.

Unfortunately, his untimely death probably hurt the nation in its recovery from the war, since Lincoln, known for both fairness and forgiveness, would probably have done a much better job of reintegrating the South than what his successors were able to accomplish. The aftermath of the war was not handled as skillfully as Lincoln might have done. Although the slaves were freed, social injustices against black Americans and racial prejudice within our society would continue to plague us for another hundred years before significant steps would finally be taken to heal some of the wounds that slavery and the war had left.

THEODORE ROOSEVELT

In the decades after Lincoln, as in those that preceded him, the country had somewhat uneventful presidencies which some historians refer to as "caretaker" administrations. Although there were issues of the day, and sometimes conflicts, America's government was by and large engrossed in "holding down the fort" and continuing the day-to-day process of survival and growth. To many, the Civil War had been a bitter lesson. We came away realizing how close we had come to collapse, and the idealism and perhaps naivete which some might previously have felt about our nation was put into question. For a while,

Theodore Roosevelt and the father of the modern environmental conservation movement, John Muir, on Glacier Point, Yosemite Valley, California

Theodore Roosevelt in "Rough Rider" Uniform (1898).

our society became more conservative, more cautious. The world was plunging headlong into the Industrial Revolution. Europe was rapidly changing, becoming friendlier and less of a threat. The country continued to expand westward. We were becoming, for the first time, not only a very large nation, but also a very powerful one and, at first, we seemed uncertain as to how to fill that role. On the surface, Theodore Roosevelt appeared to be an unlikely candidate for greatness, based on the model which previous heroes provided. Unlike Franklin or Lincoln, he was not born into poverty. He was educated at Harvard College. He was an intellectual and an advocate of strenuous physical activity. He became first a bureaucrat, and, as a New York City police commissioner, was then elected to

the New York State Assembly and served as assistant secretary of the Navy in the time leading up to the Spanish-American War.

He became governor of New York based largely on his reputation at the end of the Spanish-American War, but governed only two years before being elected vice president of the nation in 1900. When President McKinley was assassinated in 1901, Roosevelt became president, and was later elected in his own right in 1904.

Roosevelt's contribution to America is complex and involves both concrete changes in

Woodrow Wilson
1856-1924

and established food and drug inspection. Famous as an outdoorsman, Roosevelt had the foresight to provide for the preservation of America's wild spaces and was more active than any other American president, except perhaps for Franklin Roosevelt, in setting aside vast areas of federal land for conservation.

Roosevelt was also active on the international scene and helped to bring America into prominence as a world leader. Among other accomplishments, he acquired land to build the Panama Canal. While his interference in the affairs of other nations was not always commendable or successful, he helped establish the concept that America had the right to make demands on other nations and to intervene in matters that affected American security or fostered American values. Even after he left the White House, Roosevelt continued to champion socially and politically responsible government.

WOODROW WILSON

our form of government as well as more intangible contributions to the image of the American leader in the early part of the twentieth century. Under Roosevelt, the role of the presidency was strengthened. He also extended the role of government into new areas, particularly its involvement with business and the economy. Roosevelt's presidency coincided with the "rougher and meaner" phase of the Industrial Revolution, when large businesses had considerable power and did not always wield it to the public good. Roosevelt was instrumental in passing legislation that, among other things, controlled railroad fees

Admittedly, inclusion of Woodrow Wilson among the list of great American presidents again stretches that definition of some of the criteria we were previously using. As presidents went, Wilson was not overly successful. In many ways he was not highly regarded in his time, but generally the verdict of history has treated him favorably and proven that he was ahead of his time in some of his ideals and objectives.

Wilson was probably the most highly educated and intellectual man ever elected to the U.S. presidency. He graduated from

Princeton University with a law degree and Ph.D., and later became the president of that Ivy League school. He was elected governor of New Jersey in 1910, then won two presidential elections as a Democrat in 1912 and 1916.

During his first term, he carried out a variety of major reforms that were highly idealistic and won him some degree of popularity, including the Federal Reserve Act, which established America's first central banking system in 1914. However, his second term was largely consumed by the First World War in much the same way that Abraham Lincoln's presidency was consumed by the Civil War. He spent the first half of it fighting the war, and the second half trying to help the world learn from the war and prevent it from happening again. In the first objective he was successful; in the second one he was considerably less so.

Wilson's most ambitious undertaking came at the end of the war, when he became a very active and vocal member of the Versailles Peace Conference. Wilson struggled to impose principles of justice and a high moral ground upon the other nations in attendance in deciding what was to be done with the defeated Germany and the other loose ends from the war.

One of Wilson's most ambitious proposals was the League of Nations, a society organized much like the present-day United Nations, with one of its primary objectives being world peace. In the end, Wilson proved to be far more influential outside of America than within. He succeeded in getting the League of Nations adopted and started at the Versailles Conference, but failed to convince the U.S. Senate to allow the United States to

Franklin D. Roosevelt
1882-1945

join. Without America's participation, the League of Nations struggled for survival and ultimately failed.

Wilson devoted himself zealously to the cause, even going so far as to make a tour of the nation to explain the importance of the league—a tour which eventually led to his physical collapse. Although he completed his term of office, he retired from public life and was never again a strong or healthy man. He died three years later in 1924.

The primary criticism against Wilson is that he was inflexible in his idealism and he lacked political savvy—the ability to compromise when necessary and to persuade others to cooperate with him. However, Wilson is praised in much the same way but to a lesser degree than Lincoln for his whole-hearted devotion to the presidency and the well-being of the nation.

Lincoln literally gave his life when he was assassinated. Wilson effectively did the same by pushing himself to the brink of exhaustion for the causes he believed in. Wilson's ideals were not entirely lost, though it would take another bloody conflict before the American public would be fully convinced of the value of what Wilson was trying to achieve.

FRANKLIN ROOSEVELT

Roosevelt signing the Declaration of War against Japan in 1941.

Franklin Roosevelt (a distant cousin of Theodore Roosevelt) was the only American president to be elected four times (something no longer possible under American law), and his presidency presided over two extremely traumatic events in American history: the Great Depression of the 1930s and the Second World War.

Roosevelt was a distinctive individual in many ways. Like Wilson, under whom he served as assistant secretary of the Navy, he was well educated, having graduated from Harvard University and Columbia Law School. His wife, Eleanor, was likewise an intelligent and well-educated woman who played an important role both during and after his administration. Roosevelt was stricken with polio in 1921, and was disabled by this ravaging disease throughout the rest of his life. Although, during his presidency, he struggled to maintain an image of at least passable sturdiness, behind the scenes he frequently made use of a wheelchair.

He was elected governor of New York in 1928 and then defeated Herbert Hoover to become president in 1932. This was some three years after the collapse of the stock market threw the United States and much of the rest of the world into the greatest economic depression of the twentieth century. The Republicans under Hoover had been ill-prepared for the collapse. Roosevelt's Democrats inherited a extremely bleak situation, as America was weakened by massive unemployment and a shortage of key resources and was increasingly menaced by growing tensions in Europe later in the 1930s.

On the home front, Roosevelt acted aggressively to help those who were suffering most from the depression, and, in doing so, he forever changed the role of the federal government with regard to social responsibility. Roosevelt's programs were collectively known as the New Deal, and they instituted broad, sweeping relief and <u>reforms</u>, creating jobs with a variety of manpower-employing agencies and helping rebuild the U.S. economy and financial system. Although it took a long time for the country to climb out of the depression (and it didn't fully achieve this until the Second World War), most American people appreciated Roosevelt's efforts, saw some progress, and continued to support Roosevelt into his second and third terms in office.

Although Roosevelt was initially determined to keep the U.S. out of the Second World War, once our involvement became inevitable, he was an effective statesman and military leader. He mobilized industry at home for military production and helped to maintain a strong alliance with Britain and the Societ Union to keep the Allied cause united.

Although he was sometimes criticized for how he dealt with the Soviets, Roosevelt was not responsible for the aftermath of the war, since he died early in the spring of 1945. As seems so often to have been the case with American presidents, a long and difficult war took its toll on a man who had not been in the best of health to begin with. Roosevelt died on April 12, 1945. The task of ending the war and dealing with its aftermath fell to Roosevelt's vice president, Harry Truman.

Roosevelt's funeral procession with horse-drawn casket, traveling down Pennsylvania Avenue on April 24, 1945.

Chapter Three • Recap Quiz

1. In what year was George Washington elected president for the first time?

2. Who wrote Poor Richard's Almanac?

3. What was the name of Lincoln's famous document that was the first official move to free the slaves?

4. The League of Nations was an ambitious, though ultimately doomed, proposal championed by which American president?

5. What was the name given collectively to Franklin Roosevelt's social programs for dealing with the Great Depression?

ANSWERS TO QUIZ THREE

1- 1789   2- Benjamin Franklin   3- the Emancipation Proclamation

4- Woodrow Wilson   5- the New Deal

CHAPTER FOUR

THE EVOLUTION

of Our Government and Civic Life

The rights, civil liberties, and freedom of every American citizen are enshrined in law. The structure of our government, and its founding principles, are examined.

THE STATUE OF LIBERTY

The Statue of Liberty is a monumental sculpture that symbolizes freedom throughout the world. Its formal name is Liberty Enlightening the World, and it was a gift given by France in 1886. The iron frame was devised by French engineer Gustave Alexandre Eiffel, who also built the Eiffel Tower in Paris. The statue is perhaps best known for its symbolic role in greeting immigrants arriving in New York Harbor.

*The Constitution, in all its provisions,
looks to an indestructible Union composed of indestructible States.*

SALMON PORTLAND CHASE
1808-1873

Our country is the world - our countrymen are all of mankind.

WILLIAM LLOYD GARRISON
1805-1879

We must be the great arsenal of democracy.

FRANKLIN D. ROOSEVELT
1882-1945

FOUNDATION DOCUMENTS

The history of our country is a record of individual events that have:

1) affected the lives of people living in the country at the time, and also

2) left the country changed both internally and in terms of its position in the world.

Often, these are dramatic events such as wars, settlements, expansion, statehood, economic depression and so on. However, the United States as we know it today has also been shaped by a more subtle growth and refinement of our system of government, our rights as citizens, and the way we conduct ourselves publicly as voters, citizens, and taxpayers.

In this chapter, we will look specifically at government in the United States. It is often pointed out that, from a tax standpoint, an incorporated company has an identity apart from that of its owners: it can be sued, it pays its own taxes and it becomes like an actual "person" under the law. In much the same way, the United States of America is an entity which exists separate from its people. It is an institution that owns land, controls assets, and empowers political leaders with the moral and legal authority to act in conformity with very specific rules and limitations.

The United States that we know today did not suddenly spring into existence on July 4, 1776. Rather, like an enormous 225-year-old tree, it has grown and expanded well beyond its original boundaries. Some of what presently exists at the core of our national system has remained essentially unchanged since it was set in place by our Founding Fathers. However, other elements of our civic life have grown well beyond what the founders envisioned, and perhaps, arguably, in some cases even beyond what they might have

Signing of the Declaration of Independence, painting by John Trumbull in U.S. Capitol.

approved of in their original conception of the nation.

There are two concrete sources for the identity and organization of our government. The first are what can be called founding documents: the Declaration of Independence and the Constitution, including its amendments, the first ten of which are known as the Bill of Rights. We will discuss these documents in this chapter because they form the basis for everything else that has been added to them. However, there are a great many aspects of our government as it functions today that were not specifically mentioned in the founding documents. Rather, they have come about as a result of laws that have been enacted at the federal or state level. These laws have continued the ongoing process of revising the concept of America and its ways of operating on a year-by-year and administration-by-administration basis in response to the changing realities of the modern world.

Because the rights of individual states are an important part of our American system,

both criminal and civil law vary significantly from one jurisdiction to another. We will give an overview of the documents and their significance here, and highlight individual clauses or elements that are of particular significance or interest.

THE DECLARATION OF INDEPENDENCE

Once the Revolutionary War was underway and it appeared that the thirteen colonies could no longer resolve differences with England, the Continental Congress met to authorize a formal declaration of independence. Thomas Jefferson wrote the document, and Congress approved it the next day, on July 4, 1776.

In and of itself, the Declaration of Independence does little to establish an American government. It begins by asserting the rights of the American citizens to make the declaration. The opening paragraphs contain some of the world's most often quoted lines, such as, "We hold these truths to be self-evident, that all men are created equal, that they are endowed by their Creator with certain unalienable Rights, that among these are Life, Liberty and the pursuit of Happiness. That to secure these rights, Governments are instituted among Men, deriving their just Powers from the consent of the governed."

These simple sentences not only establish the framework for freedom in American society, but they also declare a fundamental right of self-government that should extend to all men everywhere. If the authority of the Declaration of Independence was to be questioned, the authors wanted to make it clear that the authority comes from the people themselves; that it is the natural right of all people to elect a government as they see fit. This was by no means a universal concept in the world of that day, though it was supported by many well-respected European philosophers.

Most of the rest of the body of the Declaration of Independence is devoted to a list of grievances against King George III of England. The Founding Fathers wanted to make absolutely clear, in the historical record, all of the reasons they had for breaking free from England. Some of the grievances

included "quartering large bodies of troops among us...cutting off our trade with parts of the world...imposing taxes on us without our consent...depriving us in many cases of the benefits of trial by jury...taking away our charters...taking away our most valuable laws, and altering fundamentally the forms of our government...suspending our own legislatures, and declaring themselves invested with power to legislate for us in all cases whatsoever."

The declaration goes on to point out how painstakingly the colonists tried to have their grievances heard and to petition for redress, pointing out that they were previously denied justice and that they consequently came to the end of their patience. It is clear that the

"Making the Flag"
Jean Louis Gerome Ferris

Declaration of Independence was being promulgated as a last resort. The king is specifically defined as a tyrant, and his tyrannical behavior was the justification for the action of the colonists.

The final paragraph of the declaration contains the fundamental status that is being declared. "That these united colonies are, and of Right ought to be, FREE AND INDEPENDENT STATES: that they are Absolved from all Allegiance to the British Crown and that all political connection between them and the State of Great Britain, is and ought to be totally dissolved; and that as Free and Independent States, they have full Power to levy War, conclude Peace, contract Alliances, establish Commerce and do all other Acts and Things which Independent States of

right do." In the final sentence, the signers of the Declaration "mutually pledge to each other our Lives, our Fortunes and our sacred Honor."

As such, the Declaration of Independence does not establish a system of government. Rather, it asserts the right to establish such a system. It is more like a "deed" stating that a country now exists and that it belongs to its people.

Nonetheless, the document is far more than an act of rebellion or a declaration of war. At the same time that it asserts our independence, it also clearly establishes our fundamental values which would be carried forward and elaborated upon at the end of the war, when it became time for the colonies to

Signing of the Civil Rights Act of 1964.

reassemble and produce a more detailed blueprint for the government of the new nation.

THE CONSTITUTION

The United States Constitution is both the blueprint and the rulebook for the United States government. It was initially drafted in 1787, and Congress declared it to be in effect in the following year, after nine of the thirteen original states formally ratified it.

Almost immediately after it was passed, Congress began the work of amending it or building new provisions into it. The first ten amendments were enacted very soon after the Constitution went into effect and came to be cumulatively known as the Bill of Rights. Other amendments have been added over the years, and the Constitution itself provides a process whereby amendments can be added at any time. However, in order for this to happen, they must first pass Congress and then be ratified by at least three-quarters of the states. This provision means that

Original copy of the Constitution of the United States.

amendments to the Constitution require substantial consensus across the country and cannot easily be passed.

The body of the Constitution contains seven articles, whose general purposes can be briefly listed as follows.

Article I—Organization, powers and procedures for the Congress, establishing the House of Representatives and the Senate.

Article II—Election, powers and duties of the president and vice president.

Article III—Powers and jurisdictions of the courts, including a Supreme Court and inferior courts to be established by Congress.

Article IV—Relations among the states and admission of new states to the union.

Article V—The processes by which the Constitution itself may be amended.

Article VI—Public debts and the supremacy of the Constitution.

Article VII—The terms by which the Constitution must be ratified.

THE AMERICAN SYSTEM OF GOVERNMENT

The federal government is composed of three branches: legislative, executive, and judicial. These branches have unique responsibilities. In simple terms, the legislative branch (Congress) passes laws, the executive branch (the president) approves laws and makes sure they are carried out, and the judicial branch (the Supreme Court) makes sure that the laws are consistent with the principles of the Constitution.

The principle behind the institution of three equal branches of government is something called the separation of powers. The framers of the Constitution were concerned that if too much power was placed in the hands of one branch, the government would resemble a monarchy (like Britain) and be disloyal to the will of the people.

The first four articles of the Constitution have established the framework for our system of government, and these have not changed significantly since the Constitution was first adopted. The following paragraphs summarize the present system and structure of our federal government and how it interacts on the most fundamental levels.

The United States Congress is composed of two houses, the House of Representatives and the Senate. The Senate is designed to give equal power to all of the states, regardless of their size or population. Two senators are elected from each state. The term of office for a senator is six years.

The House of Representatives is structured very differently. It is designed to give greater representation to those states with larger populations. Over the years, the number of members of the House of Representatives has changed from time to time, and congressional districts for representatives are reassessed and reapportioned as shifts occur in the relative distribution of people across the country. Some states may have twenty or thirty representatives, others only a handful, depending on their relative populations. All members of the House of Representatives (435 in total today) serve for two years; thus, they are all up for reelection in every even-numbered year.

The President of the United States is elected by the people. A presidential election occurs every four years. An election is held in November and a newly elected president assumes office in January. Between the time of the election and the "inauguration," the former president remains in office.

At the time the Constitution was first enacted, there were no limits on the number of terms which a president could hold. However, in more recent times, the 22nd Amendment to the Constitution imposed a two-term limit on the presidency, in keeping with the precedent of George Washington.

The U.S. Capitol, where Congress convenes, in Washington, D.C.

The vice president is now (not originally) elected along with the president, and assumes office in the event that the president should die or leave office before the end of his term. The vice president also presides over the Senate and is allowed to cast a vote in that legislature if there should be a tie.

The Constitution also establishes a Supreme Court, which has authority over all other courts in the country, both state and federal. Cases from lower courts may be appealed to the Supreme Court, and any cases involving the constitutionality of laws may be brought to the Supreme Court, where laws can be challenged if it is believed they do not conform with the provisions of the Constitution. Frequently in our history the Supreme Court has thrown out a state or federal law by declaring it "unconstitutional," meaning that, in enacting it, the Congress or state legislature exceeded their power or jurisdiction as defined under the Constitution. This establishes the Constitution as the overriding document in American justice. No laws can be enacted that differ from the Constitution or contradict or negate any of its provisions, as interpreted by the Supreme Court.

One of the most ingenious and admired aspects of the American system of government is that, from the very beginning, the Founding Fathers built into it what is known as a system of "checks and balances." Despite their enthusiasm at giving birth to a new nation and its high ideals, they nonetheless managed to be level-headed and almost cynical in their assessment of politicians and the possibility of politicians being corrupted by power and influence. They wanted to be sure their country had a system that would protect it against a broad range of possible scenarios, including incompetency or attempts by one member or group within the government to subvert the process or to act in ways which were not in the best interests of the public.

Thus, not one of the three branches of our federal government — Congress, the president, or the Supreme Court — has absolute power. Laws are passed by Congress, but they must be approved or signed into law by the president. The president has the authority to veto laws if he does not approve of them or if he thinks they are not in the best interests of the public. When the president vetoes a law, it is refused and sent back to the Congress. However, this does not necessarily mean that the law is dead. It is possible for the Congress to vote on the law once again: if a two-thirds majority is obtained in both houses, this overrides the president's veto. However, in order to pass it a second time after a veto, a greater majority of votes are needed. This ensures that Congress must stand firm behind the law if it is to be enacted without the president's approval.

Even when both Congress passes and the president signs laws, the Supreme Court has the right to invalidate them by deciding that

they are unconstitutional. However, even the Supreme Court does not necessarily have the last word, because the Constitution provides a process whereby the Constitution itself can be amended. If the Supreme Court decides that the federal government does not have the authority to do something, and Congress is intent on doing it anyway, Congress can assume that authority by passing an amendment to the Constitution and having it ratified by three-quarters of the states. Once having done that, the Supreme Court will no longer be in a position to declare the law unconstitutional. However, bear in mind that, as mentioned earlier, changing the Constitution is not an easy matter. It requires approval by Congress and then ratification by three quarters of the state legislatures.

The constitution clearly divides the powers of the federal government into legislative, executive, and judicial branches. It also establishes a division between federal and state powers. The Founding Fathers of our country were big believers in states' rights. There was a great deal of difference in lifestyle and viewpoint among the original colonies—for example, about slavery. There was often a very different way of thinking in Virginia than in Pennsylvania or New York. When the colonies agreed to merge, they did not want to become one giant entity that no longer preserved state boundaries and traditions. Furthermore, they did not want all power and authority to lie with the federal government. Were this not the case, if one region of the country disapproved or wanted to do things differently, it would have no power to do so if it were outvoted by the majority in the rest of the country.

Consequently, provision was made for establishing certain elements which fell under federal rights and under federal jurisdiction, and others which were under state jurisdiction. These concepts have been refined and somewhat altered over the years, but the fundamental principle remains intact from the beginning.

We can briefly sketch some of the powers that lie at each level of government. The federal government has the power to raise an army, go to war, and enact trade agreements with other nations. It also looks after matters that extend beyond state lines, such as interstate transportation. The states, on the other hand, have the ability to look after a great many matters that affect day-to-day elements of public life, including social services, education, public works (state highways, bridges, etc.) and the establishment and regulation of local city and county governments. The states also have their own courts and are able to pass their own laws concerning a broad range of civil and criminal matters. Although there are many similarities between the laws of one state and another with regard to both civil and criminal issues, there are some significant differences from state to state. Some activities are legal in some states and not in others. Furthermore, penalties vary significantly from one part of the country to another. Some states still use the death penalty for certain crimes, whereas others have abolished the death penalty and use life imprisonment as the most severe punishment.

Both levels of government can impose taxes of certain types, and there are also several other areas where, in practice, there is some overlap between activities on state and federal levels.

THE GROWTH OF GOVERNMENT

It is important to understand how dramatically both the state and federal governments have grown over the years. In the early days of our nation the role of government was much smaller than what it has become today. There was no income tax, for example. Taxes were assessed on some specific activities such as sales of goods, import duties and so on. Indeed, it took a special amendment to the Constitution, the 16th Amendment in 1913, to authorize the government to impose income taxes.

From the beginning, the federal government has maintained a military and enacted treaties with Native Americans, territories, and foreign governments. Initially, the government had relatively little to do with regulating business within the country or with social programs and conditions. There was no welfare system or unemployment insurance. There were no laws protecting workers or banning unsafe practices. Laws were quickly enacted to designate serious crimes, but the wide range of activities that are presently outlawed or regulated has emerged gradually over many decades of interactions between Congress, the courts, and state legislatures and governors.

As needs have arisen, governments have enacted laws to deal with new problems and to

President Richard Nixon's second term in office (left to right): Secretary of State Henry Kissinger, Nixon, Vice President Gerald Ford, and Chief of Staff Alexander Haig.

protect citizens in light of specific issues at hand. Eventually, it became necessary to control big business and to set labor standards. Labor law exists under the federal and state levels, depending upon the aspect involved. It became necessary to define and protect the rights of citizens (and better define who qualified as "citizens"). It became necessary to protect the environment and to designate lands for public use. It became necessary to regulate transportation and highways, particularly in the age of automobiles, both for the public's safety and to create and maintain transportation systems, including highway, railway, and airport transportation. As life

became more complicated, government and law became more complicated.

Today, there are wide ranging laws affecting business practices, taxation, protection against discrimination, and attempts at protection against invasion of privacy. Even criminal law is continuously being redefined. The founding fathers did not create laws against child pornography, drunk driving, or stock market fraud. However, the authority to enact laws on all of these issues, and the limitations on that authority, were implicit in the Constitution and the amendments that grew from it.

THE BILL OF RIGHTS

In the preceding paragraphs, mention was given to amendments made to the Constitution. While it is not necessary to list all of the amendments here, it should be noted that some things we take for granted about our rights as citizens today arose not out of the original Constitution itself, but in amendments made at later dates.

The abolition of slavery, which began as the Emancipation Proclamation signed by Abraham Lincoln, became the 13th Amendment to the Constitution in 1865. The right of all males to vote, regardless of race or color, was stated in the 15th Amendment. It was not until the 19th Amendment that the right to vote was extended to women. Initially, not all senators were elected by the people; the 17th Amendment made this a requirement.

Interestingly, some amendments to the Constitution proved to be of limited effectiveness or were outright mistakes. The 18th Amendment prohibited alcohol across the nation. When Prohibition led to more problems than solutions, the 21st Amendment was enacted to repeal the 18th Amendment.

The original ten amendments that make up the Bill of Rights are the shining jewels of our Constitution. They embody our fundamental rights and freedoms as American citizens. The Bill of Rights, more than any other document, has served as America's model to the world of what a free and democratic society should be. The freedoms

granted in these amendments state:

I. Freedom of religion, speech, assembly and freedom of the press.

II. The right to keep and bear arms.

III. Provisions protecting citizens against having to quarter soldiers.

IV. Security from unreasonable searches and seizures.

V. The rights of the accused to due process under law and to plead against self-incrimination.

VI. The rights of the accused before and during trial, and to a speedy trial.

VII. The right to a trial by jury in civil cases.

VIII. Provision to prohibit excessive bail and fines and to prohibit cruel and unusual punishment.

IX, X. The final two amendments of the Bill

of Rights reserve unenumerated rights to the people and of the states. Their effect is to proclaim that, although a right may not be stated in the Constitution, it can nonetheless exist. Also, if a right is not specifically granted to the federal government by the Constitution, and if the Constitution does not specifically prohibit the states from having such a right, then the states will have rights in those areas. In other words, all powers that are not specifically granted to the federal government or specifically prohibited to the states fall under the category of states' rights.

Although the Bill of Rights is very clear in its provisions, interpreting or enforcing the Bill of Rights has been an exceedingly complex and difficult question throughout history. Court cases today continue to turn upon judicial interpretation of constitutional amendments. For example, freedom of the press and the right to free speech are provided for in the 1st Amendment. In practice, the courts must determine what reasonable limitations there are to such rights. For example, while people have the right to speak their mind, they do not have the right to incite others to overthrow the government, nor do they have the right to incite others to hate crimes or to use the right of speech to slander or defame another person's reputation unjustly.

The press has the right to report the truth to the people, with specific limitations. For example, the courts may impose a restriction on the right of the press to report certain information about a case being tried. For national security reasons, the government has the right to deny certain information from being given to the press or to keep the press from reporting it.

The 4th Amendment has also provoked a variety of special concerns. This amendment protects against unreasonable searches and seizures, but the term "unreasonable" is open to interpretation. Laws have been established to define the precise manner in which searches of persons, homes, or vehicles may be conducted by police during an investigation or an arrest.

The 2nd Amendment to the Constitution remains one of the most contentious. This Amendment gives citizens the right to bear arms (meaning guns and other weapons). While all fundamental rights foreseen in the Bill of Rights are still as applicable today as they were more than two hundred years ago, some would argue that 2nd Amendment rights no longer make sense in today's world. With the many problems that illegal or imprudent use of firearms have caused in our society, certain groups within the country would like to see the 2nd Amendment repealed or altered. In practice, the federal government has restricted certain types of weapons, but there has never been a serious attempt to make it illegal for ordinary citizens to own weapons. As there is such strong feeling about this matter, it is unlikely that this right will ever be taken away from American citizens. The government may impose more and more restrictions, but the right to bear arms goes back to colonial times and is an important and lasting part of our heritage. However, the government nonetheless punishes those who use firearms illegally.

It is interesting to note that several items in the Bill of Rights deal with how persons accused of crimes must be brought to justice. These provisions sprang from widespread abuse of the courts and prison systems that were common in other parts of the world in the eighteenth century. Prisoners were often subjected to unfair trials, beaten, tortured, subjected to harsh punishments, held in jail without bail for long periods of time awaiting trial, or subjected to other abuses. The Bill of Rights allowed for a judicial system whereby persons accused of crimes are presumed innocent until found guilty, and where they are given rights to a fair trial and to humane treatment both before and after being convicted.

1. What is the name commonly given to the first ten amendments to the U.S. Constitution?

2. Fill in the blanks in the following famous quotation from the Declaration of Independence: "We hold these truths to be self-evident, that all men are created equal, that they are endowed by their Creator with certain unalienable Rights, that among these are _____ , _____ , and the pursuit of _____ ."

3. How many articles are contained in the body of the U.S. Constitution?

4. In order to be passed in spite of a presidential veto, a law must receive the approval of at least _____ of the members of the House of Representatives and the same majority in the Senate.

5. Freedom of speech, religion, and the press are all guaranteed by which amendment to the Constitution?

ANSWERS TO QUIZ FOUR

1- the Bill of Rights   2- Life, Liberty, Happiness   3- seven

4- 2/3   5- the First Amendment

AMERICAN HISTORY

Since 1945

Since the end of
World War II, the
United States has established
itself as a global superpower
while facing the challenges of
an ever-changing social
landscape within its
own borders.

WASHINGTON MEMORIAL

Washington Monument, national memorial authorized in 1848. Located in Washington, D.C., at the western end of the National Mall, this four-sided stone structure honors George Washington, the first president of the United States (1789-1797). The monument was modeled after a classic Egyptian obelisk. It is 555 feet high and is one of the tallest masonry structures in the world.

Some people call me an idealist. Well, that is the way I know I am an American. America is the only idealistic nation in the world.

WOODROW WILSON
1856-1924

America is a system of rugged individualism.

HERBERT HOOVER
1874-1964

While our country's history is important, we do not expect our students to place equal emphasis on all events in our nation's history. From a practical standpoint, it is more important to understand the most significant historical events and then focus on more recent events. Recent events aren't necessarily more important, but they do have a more immediate impact on our lives. They are also events that people still alive today have lived through and experienced. Knowledge of these events is not theoretical or supplemental. Knowledge of recent history is considered essential to being a well-rounded member of our society. In the following section, we will take you on a chronological journey from the end of World War II through the present day.

AMERICAN HISTORY SINCE 1945

America's involvement in World War II was administered by President Roosevelt; but, since Roosevelt died in office, it was President Harry Truman who was responsible for dropping the bombs on Japan that ended the conflict. While the country was understandably elated and relieved to be free of the dangers and uncertainties of such a massive and devastating war, it was almost immediately faced with new problems. The returning soldiers swelled the ranks of the workforce, and not everyone was able to find employment or housing. Woman and African Americans, who made vital contributions to the war effort, once again faced limited opportunities. Many industries that had been geared towards wartime production of supplies and weapons were no longer needed, and the peacetime economy struggled at first to meet consumers' demands.

Furthermore, we fought World War II with an uneasy alliance with countries like the Soviet Union, whose communist government we distrusted. It had been necessary to form this alliance in order to defeat our mutual enemies. After the war, we began to see Russia, along with Communist China, as our new enemies. This was fueled by the fact that after the Allied forces advanced on Berlin at the end of the war, the Russian troops failed to withdraw from the countries they crossed. Instead, they forcibly absorbed them into their communist system, creating "puppet states" with leaders who were answerable to Moscow. Thus, for all of these reasons and others, America had relatively little time to relax before it once again felt the threat of impending crisis.

What aggravated the situation was the very device that saved us at the end of the war: the atomic bomb. Besides the United States, several other countries had been working on the bomb. The Soviet Union, in 1949, developed nuclear weapons of its own. Now that we were adversaries of this superpower, we soon came to realize that these weapons of mass destruction were likely aimed at us and we felt we had to be prepared to defend ourselves from the possibility of a devastating attack, which many believed to be inevitable.

Tensions with communist countries rapidly escalated. President Truman was succeeded by Republican Dwight Eisenhower, a war hero who had served in Europe. Under Truman and Eisenhower, the United States became involved in the Korean War, as previously discussed. Asia was being split between capitalist and communist ideologies, and communism was gradually spreading to more and more territory. Indeed, among many of its leaders, there was an avowed and outspoken intent to force communism upon as much of the world as possible. This not only heightened the tension between ourselves and Russia and China, but it led us to gear up for military interventions in Asia and other parts of the world, such as Latin America and Lebanon.

Fear of communism reached a fevered pitch in the early 1950s. Not only was the country moving to resist communism on foreign soil, but a movement was underway in the United States to expose communist sympathizers and attack liberals in American media, labor unions, and even Hollywood film stars and producers. A great many innocent people were targeted and called to testify before the House Un-American Activities Commission in Congress.

Eisenhower was, on the whole, a rather popular president, though his administration did not institute many significant domestic policies. The war effort in Korea was modestly successful and the president's firm but patient approach to dealing with the communist threat was generally supported.

At home, society was changing. The economy was booming and families were growing. Thanks to the growing availability of the automobile and the construction of new highways, middle-class suburbs sprouted around major American cities. Meanwhile,

Dwight D. Eisenhower served as Supreme Commander of the Allied Forces in Europe during World War II. As President, his long list of accomplishments include ending the Korean War, the creation of the Interstate Highway System, and maintaining peace with the Soviet Union during the beginning of what was later termed the "Cold War"

racial tensions were escalating as African Americans became more outspoken in their demands for equal rights. As well, many young intellectuals and artists were critical of the conformity they perceived in society and the authoritative government that supported it.

This led to an interesting presidential election in 1960. The Republicans put forth Richard Nixon, who had served as Eisenhower's vice president. The Democrats nominated a young but charismatic leader named John F. Kennedy, a senator from Massachusetts who had also been a war hero. Kennedy won a narrow victory by promising "to get the country moving again," to remain tough against Communism, and to work for greater justice and opportunity at home.

Shortly into Kennedy's term of office, however, the Cold War (as the tensions with Communist nations had come to be known)

came to a head with the Cuban Missile Crisis of October 1962. At that time, Fidel Castro, the communist president of Cuba, was the only communist leader in the Americas. The United States, which had always been friendly with the Cuban people, made ill-fated attempts to help overthrow him. The Russians, on the other hand, wholeheartedly supported Castro and moved nuclear missiles to Cuba, where they could be aimed at the United States in case war should erupt between the two superpowers.

President Kennedy took a firm stand against Russian Premier Khrushchev. Publicly, Khrushchev made a dramatic gesture of retreat and agreed to remove the missiles, which greatly enhanced Kennedy's image and popularity. Privately, it became known many years later that Khrushchev was offered significant concessions in return, such as the withdrawal of U.S. missiles from Turkey.

Lyndon Baines Johnson taking the oath of office on Air Force One, shortly after the assassination of John F. Kennedy on November 22, 1963.

While the crisis raged, many Americans built fallout shelters in their basements, convinced that a nuclear war between both countries was about to erupt.

Kennedy's administration also moved to enfranchise the young people of the country and get them interested in political and social activism, as well as support the growing movement for civil rights for black Americans (despite some initial reluctance). Unfortunately, as it would turn out, President Kennedy, still a firm anti-Communist, also acted to initiate and escalate the involvement of American troops in Vietnam.

President Kennedy was assassinated in Dallas, Texas, on November 22, 1963, after serving less than three years of his term in office. He was replaced by Vice President Lyndon Johnson, a Texan who had been added to the Kennedy ticket because he was more conservative by nature and more likely to attract southern voters. Nonetheless, Johnson, an old "New Dealer," committed himself to supporting many of Kennedy's liberal causes. He worked vigorously on behalf of civil rights legislation, to the point of alienating many of his southern supporters. He launched what he called his "War on Poverty" to improve the standard of living and social conditions of poor and working-class Americans. He also backed America's military commitment in Vietnam, which, under his administration, escalated from a sporadic conflict into a full-scale war.

The Vietnam War became so unpopular among young people and liberal-minded Americans that it ultimately led to the downfall of President Johnson. After being elected by a landslide to his own presidential term in 1964, his popularity rapidly deteriorated, and he didn't run again in 1968. By that time, the country was torn apart with civil unrest and ideological differences. Conflict between blacks and whites had led to violence and rioting in many cities around the country. Many young people were dropping out and rebelling against organized society, advancing a lifestyle which included experimentation with sex and drugs, devotion to protest music, and demonstrations, sometimes violent ones, in an attempt to end the Vietnam War.

In the election of 1968, after John Kennedy's younger brother Robert was assassinated while campaigning, the Democratic Party chose to nominate Vice-President Hubert Humphrey to run in place of Lyndon Johnson. The Republicans came back with Richard Nixon, the man who had lost to John Kennedy eight years earlier. This time, the country, fed up with the failure of many Democratic policies and the continuing war, not to mention the domestic problems it was causing at home, believed that Nixon provided the best chance for a swift and "honorable" end to the conflict and reestablishment of "law and order" at home.

Nixon discovered the War in Vietnam was not as easy to bring to an end as he had hoped, and he soon found himself being attacked much like his predecessor, Johnson, for not only continuing but escalating and broadening the conflict. It took most of Nixon's term of office to finally effect a peace treaty, with the help of Secretary of State Henry Kissinger,

Robert Kennedy first gained national recognition for his aggressive investigation of suspected underworld involvement in the Teamsters Union. However, as Attorney General, he became synonymous with the civil rights movement.

with the North Vietnamese. Kissinger was also instrumental in the most enduring contribution of the Nixon administration: the beginning of diplomatic and trading relations with Russia and China.

Richard Nixon won a landslide victory for a second term of office in 1972, despite dissent over Vietnam. He had not served long into his second term when he was forced to resign on August 9, 1974, due to a scandal (now called "Watergate") involving illegal campaign activities. Nixon chose to resign rather than face an impeachment trial. Although he was perhaps not directly involved in illegal activity, his dishonesty about what he knew and his blatant attempts to cover up and obstruct an investigation into the matter rapidly sapped his public image and popularity and caused overwhelming opposition to mount against him in Congress. Nixon was replaced by his vice president, Gerald Ford, who served out the rest of the term. Ironically, Ford had become vice president under the terms of the 25th Amendment when Nixon's original vice president, Spiro Agnew, was forced to resign over a different scandal.

The 1970s was an uneasy decade for America. The economy remained sluggish, largely due to an oil crisis, with only brief cycles of limited improvement. We still faced the threat of communist expansion, and continued to pour huge amounts of resources into building a giant military complex that we hoped would protect us. Much of the idealism of the '60s had faded, along with the hopes for significant change and improvement. Certainly, some advances were made, particularly in civil rights, but by and large the poor remained poor and America faced the same internal conflicts and tensions, only this time with more cynicism.

A general sense of dissatisfaction and disillusionment with the Republicans as a result of the Watergate scandals, coupled with economic problems and frustration with the progress of social reform, help set the stage for Jimmy Carter, the Democratic presidential candidate in 1976. Carter, a former Georgia governor and naval officer, campaigned in part on a promise of a more efficient and responsible government, and honesty and integrity.

By any objective standards, the Carter administration was a disappointment, although he was instrumental in achieving peace between Egypt and Israel. Little was accomplished by way of improving the domestic situation, which featured tremendous inflation. A couple of international incidents hurt American prestige abroad and created an image of Carter as a weak leader.

By this point in time, tensions between the United States and parts of the Arab world were deepening, not only because of ideological differences but also in disagreements on how to manage the world's dwindling supplies of oil and petroleum reserves. When the Arab countries, together with the other oil-producing countries of the world, instituted an effort to drive up oil prices, the United States economy was ill prepared. This led to an economic downturn in the United States and elsewhere in the world, one which also affected American citizens very directly. Sometimes fights would break out at the long line-ups at gas pumps when supplies became limited and prices rapidly climbed.

However, it was an incident not directly related to the energy crisis that doomed the Carter administration. Islamic revolutionaries in Iran seized the U.S. embassy and took over sixty Americans hostage to retaliate for America's support of the overthrown Iranian shah (king). A military effort to free them was bungled when U.S. helicopters were caught in a desert dust storm and crashed. Americans, already frustrated with the situation at home, now felt embarrassed that their military was losing its capability to function effectively.

Ronald Reagan implemented policies that reversed trends toward greater government involvement in economic and social regulation. He also brought in a new style of presidential leadership, downgrading the role of the president as an administrator and increasing the importance of communication via national news media. He was the oldest person ever to serve as president.

The brief and ill-fated return of the Democrats to power set up a long era of stable Republican presidency which extended through two terms of President Ronald Reagan and one of his vice president, George H.W. Bush (though the Republicans did not always control Congress during that time.) The Republican years were characterized by relative peace in the world, although the Cold War struggle between the United States and Russia continued and caused both nations to build up considerable nuclear stockpiles and conventional military capabilities. While the Reagan administration was frequently criticized for the amount of spending on defense, the cornerstone of the Republican ideology was always to remain firm in opposition to communism and to protect the United States from possible attack by its enemies. By and large, the American people accepted this explanation, although

deteriorating conditions for America's poor caused some opposition and ill feeling towards the Republicans in power.

Even after the oil crisis, the United States remained in a long economic recession. The federal deficits grew, unemployment remained relatively high, and growth was relatively slow. The Republican response to economic problems came to be called (mainly by its critics) the "trickle-down theory." In essence, this theory proposed that by offering tax cuts to big business and creating as favorable a climate for American industry as possible, it would lead to the kind of economic growth that would eventually create jobs and better incomes for average Americans.

The Republican philosophy did not advocate giving welfare to the poor. Relatively little was done to advance or improve the plight of America's inner cities. Most liberal-minded groups in the country were upset with the Republicans for one reason or another. Environmentalists complained because part of the Republican strategy for stimulating the economy relaxed previously tough anti-pollution and conservation laws, since these laws seemed to interfere with the ability of resource industries to expand their operations and turn enough of a profit to make further investment attractive to them.

The Reagan and Bush administrations also took a hardline against crime and drugs, implementing tougher laws and severe penalties that placed more people in jail without alleviating the underlying causes of the problems or significantly reducing their impact. President Reagan in particular took a tough verbal stance against legalization of abortion and was slow to act in support of other "liberal" causes, such as women's issues and gay rights.

Despite his stubbornly conservative stand on some of these issues, history shows that President Reagan was one of the most popular American leaders since Eisenhower. He was seen, at least by conservatives, as an honest and sincere man who genuinely cared about the welfare of the nation. Some of his economic policies were not as successful as he would have liked. When Reagan was first elected, there were fears among many Americans that the ultra-conservative element of the Republican Party would aggravate tensions with the Soviet Union, China, and other traditionally hostile countries. By the end of Reagan's administration, not only were relations between the United States and the Soviet Union better than they had been in

many years, but under Premier Mikhail Gorbachev, Russia was on the verge of abandoning the communist system altogether.

Reagan's popularity helped George H.W. Bush to be elected in 1988. Bush's administration was characterized by holding the line on many of Reagan's policies and programs. However, it was interrupted by a significant crisis when Saddam Hussein, the president of Iraq, invaded and took control of Kuwait, a move triggered in part by ongoing tension over oil between the U.S. and the Arab nations. The United States, acting with several other allied nations, launched the Gulf War, from 1990 to 1991, in order to liberate Kuwait as well as limit the power and weapons capability of Saddam Hussein, a sworn enemy of both the United States and Israel, one of America's allies in the region.

The Gulf War was a military success, but it left a wake of controversy that diminished George Bush's popularity. Many were critical that Bush liberated Kuwait but did not continue the war effort long enough to capture Saddam Hussein or drive him from power. Ten years later, Hussein would still be in power and the United States would once again find itself taking military action.

Bill Clinton's first presidential election victory came in part because Americans were gravely concerned about the nation's economy, which had been in a recession for much of George Bush's presidency.

Another source of controversy during the Gulf War had to do with American casualties, particularly concerning servicemen who claimed to suffer from undetermined exposure to chemicals or biological warfare agents. Many servicemen returning from the war became ill, months or even years afterwards. Although the causes of many of these illnesses remain controversial, many felt that they had not received adequate protection or information from their own government.

Bush's term was also tainted by a tax hike and an economic recession. By the end of his first term of office, it was becoming clear that Americans were willing to consider the possibility of change. Twelve years of Republican rule failed to resolve important domestic problems, reduce the debt, or make life much better for low-income or working-class Americans. When the young Arkansas

Governor Bill Clinton won the presidential election of 1992, he reminded America of the happier and certainly more idealistic days of John Kennedy.

Many historians believe it unfair to evaluate the contribution of any American president in terms of the country's economic performance during his administration without looking at the entire global situation. The Republican presidents struggled at a time when most of the Western world was struggling. By contrast, during the two terms of the Clinton presidency, the United States, along with much of the Western world, made dramatic gains in improving its economic climate, reforming some important social programs and eliminating the deficit that plagued the federal government and restricted its abilities to initiate new programs. Historians debate how much personal credit

Clinton deserves for this dramatic upturn, but it is a fact nonetheless that he enjoyed high approval ratings with the American public.

In the early 1990s, the Soviet Union finally gave up Communism and ceased to be a constant threat to Americans, allowing both countries to devote less money to defense spending and more to reforming their domestic situations. Several key trade agreements were either initiated or expanded as the Western world moved more toward a global economy, where countries steadily abandoned trade practices that isolated them and inhibited free competition.

Bill Clinton would put his personal popularity to the test in a series of scandals that shook his presidency and came close to toppling it. At the time he was governor of Arkansas, he became involved in business dealings that were criticized and investigated, although charges were never laid. However, he did face lawsuits and, eventually, a grand jury investigation as a result of accusations of sexual harassment or impropriety that were brought against him. The most famous of these was the Monica Lewinsky case. She was a young White House intern with whom the president had engaged in a sexual relationship. At first, Clinton denied that there had been an improper relationship, but later admitted to it and apologized both to Ms. Lewinsky and to the American people. At the time this became public, there had been a determined effort underway for several years by the Republicans to investigate the president and find a means of discrediting him and removing him from office. Some Republican Congress members alleged that the president had committed

crimes by lying to the grand jury and obstructing justice in trying to encourage others to lie with regard to the Lewinsky affair and other matters. Despite the fact that most of the American public continued to support the President and accepted his public apology, the Republicans in Congress pushed to have the president impeached. The House passed an impeachment resolution and a trial was conducted in the Senate, as provided for in the Constitution. The trial resulted in President Clinton's acquittal. The House prosecutors were not able to win the required majority of Senate votes they would need to remove Clinton from office.

With the rest of his second term now safe, the President once again turned his attention toward continuing to manage the country's internal and foreign affairs problem, though he was distracted by the impeachment process. Saddam Hussein remained an adversary and military strikes were once again ordered on Iraq, this time on a more limited basis, in order to destroy some of Saddam's weapons capabilities. The United States also took an active role in intervening militarily in Yugoslavia to help bring an end to violence that had led to numerous atrocities being committed against ethnic minorities in Kosovo. At home, the country continued to show good economic performance. Both political parties began to prepare themselves for the election that would produce the first presidency of the twenty-first century.

The presidential election of 2000 matched Texas Governor George W. Bush, son of the former president, against Al Gore, the sitting vice president. It would go down as one of the closest and most contested elections in American history. For more than a month after Election Day, election officials in the state of Florida counted and recounted ballots to determine which candidate had won the state and could thus win enough electoral votes to be elected outright. Finally, with Bush holding onto a very narrow lead, the Supreme Court ruled that the recount process being used was unconstitutional and that the recount must stop. Bush was declared the winner and was sworn in a month later amid lingering controversy about the fairness of the election.

Less than a year into Bush's first term as president, a massive terrorist attack was carried out on September 11, 2001. Militant Islamists loyal to Osama bin Laden's al-Qaeda network hijacked four passenger airliners and flew them into buildings, destroying the World Trade Center in New York City and causing the deaths of nearly 3,000 people. The nation felt horrified by the attacks, yet united in a renewed feeling of patriotism. President Bush responded by declaring war on terrorism and initiating an international coalition of forces to invade Afghanistan, the country where bin Laden was believed to be hiding. Allied troops successfully destroyed al-Qaeda camps and removed the Taliban regime that had provided a safe haven for terrorist training, though bin Laden remained at large and peace in the country would be difficult to maintain.

Still traumatized from 9/11, the U.S. came to acknowledge that neither oceans nor treaties would keep it safe. Bush gathered support for the notion that a preemptive war against Iraq was necessary to protect America from another devastating attack. In March 2003, the U.S. led an invasion to depose dictator Saddam Hussein and prevent him from using weapons of mass destruction. Less than two months after the war began, the Iraqi army was defeated, and Saddam and his ruling party were removed from the government.

The U.S. was not, however, prepared for the chaos in Iraq that would develop following the initial invasion. As competing militias carried out frequent attacks against American troops and the fragile Iraqi government that the U.S. attempted to support, Americans at home began to lose faith in President Bush and question whether the war had been worth its cost. In the first five years of the war, about 4,000 American troops would lose their lives, and hundreds of billions of dollars would be spent on a war that, like Vietnam, seemed not to be fulfilling its initial purposes of preserving peace and democracy.

Because of the continued struggle in Iraq, as well as the government's perceived mishandling of New Orleans following Hurricane Katrina in 2005, public support for Bush declined significantly during his second term in office. Although it is too soon to properly assess Bush's place in history, it is clear that the end result of the Iraq War will greatly affect how he will be remembered.

Chapter Five • Recap Quiz

1. Which country was the second to develop an atomic bomb?

2. Which U.S. president took a firm stance during the Cuban Missile Crisis?

3. Who launched what he called his "War on Poverty"?

4. What was the name of the scandal that caused President Nixon to resign?

5. Name a cause that President Reagan strongly advocated, and one that he strongly opposed.

6. What nation took dozens of Americans hostage in 1979, damaging President Carter's popularity and chances of being reelected?

6- Iran

5- advocated tough stance against crime and drugs, opposed abortion

1- Russia   2- John F. Kennedy   3- Lyndon Johnson   4- Watergate

ANSWERS TO QUIZ FIVE

IMPORTANT AMERICANS

in Civilian Life

While countless individuals have made important contributions to the American way of life and the destiny of our nation, there are those who left a legacy that will live forever.

WHITE HOUSE

White House, official residence of the president of the U.S., built in its original form between 1792 and 1800, and situated at 1600 Pennsylvania Ave. in Washington, D.C. Known variously through its history as the President's Palace, the President's House, and the Executive Mansion, the building has always been most popularly known as the White House. This designation became official in 1901, when Theodore Roosevelt had the name engraved on his stationery. It has been the home of every president in American history with the exception of George Washington, who approved the act that led to its construction. Although the White House has been subject to numerous renovations and additions, it has retained its classically simple character.

I have a dream that one day this nation will rise up, live out the true meaning of its creed: we hold these truths to be self-evident, that all men are created equal.

MARTIN LUTHER KING
1929-1968

It is important to realize that the United States has not grown into the leading nation that it is today through the achievements of only its presidents. There are also a great many civilian Americans and significant events that have helped shape who we have become as a people and changed our way of life and that of the rest of the world.

When we discussed our great presidents, we began by questioning the concept of greatness. It is clearly a subjective term. A person can be a hero in some people's eyes and a villain in others. We suggested greatness could be measured in terms of the impact that presidents had on the country, and the degree to which they were able to make lasting changes.

In this final section, we will use this same yardstick to profile six prominent civilian Americans who played important roles in our history. Even more so than with the presidents, it is no simple task to select a mere handful from among the many Americans who have made important contributions. It is impossible to pick the best or the most important without slighting others of equal importance. Indeed, it is unlikely that any two historians would agree completely on the short list of names profiled in this section.

Nonetheless, there is value in learning about individual lives and, in particular, in looking at the patterns by which these individuals were able to influence the society around them. After all, what we are doing here is not merely studying the facts and details, but also acquiring an understanding of the process. From that point of view, even looking at a few isolated examples can be very useful in giving us a sense of what it means to be an American and how we have come to be what we are today.

Many Americans feel pride in our country. While almost everyone acknowledges that there are still problems and injustices in our society, we are nonetheless highly respected throughout much of the world for our freedom, our standard of living, our values, our ingenuity, competitiveness, and our will to succeed. We have created a society that is far from perfect, yet human rights and the quality of life here are as highly respected as they are anywhere in the world today. It is important to understand, however, that this did not develop automatically. It took the contributions of many individual Americans to gradually move us closer and closer to the standards and values we enjoy today. Furthermore, in almost every case, the heroes of American history encountered opposition — indeed, sometimes the opposition was so strong that it threatened or even cost them their lives.

The story of the building of America is largely a story of individual courage. People looked around them and saw that things were not the way they ought to be or not as good as they could be, and they were brave enough to stand up for something new and better.

In all societies—and ours is no exception—there is often a great resistance to change. People are set in their ways. They are defensive about their beliefs and their actions. It is often extremely difficult to get individuals, let alone society as a whole, to change their perspective, particularly concerning fundamental moral issues. Nonetheless, this is exactly what has happened several times in our history in regard to such issues as slavery, civil rights, racial tolerance, social responsibility, compassion for the poor and the willingness to help others in the world.

The following important Americans are presented in no particular order, not even chronologically. There are no attempts to establish a hierarchy of importance. Indeed, if anything, the order has been selected to demonstrate the diversity of backgrounds from which important Americans have arisen. Because diversity is an important theme here, we will attempt to show a variety of ethnic backgrounds. Likewise, the fields to which the individuals contributed are diverse. If there is a message here it is simply this: in this country, much is possible. A person with an original and meaningful idea, willing to expend a considerable amount of effort, has a chance at

achieving prominence or even greatness. But we must remember that, for everyone who does achieve fame, there are many millions of hard-working Americans whose names will never be mentioned in any history book, and who have helped to further the cause and solidify the contributions begun by others.

MARTIN LUTHER KING

Slavery tainted more than two hundred years of our nation's history, and the circumstances under which it was abolished led to another hundred years of prejudice, segregation, discrimination, and uneasiness between the races. Eventually, this went on for so long that many blacks and whites accepted it as the status quo, believing that it would probably always be characteristic of our nation.

From time to time, people of both races emerged who felt that this was not good enough and believed in the possibility of meaningful change. Perhaps the most famous of all was Dr. Martin Luther King, a black Baptist minister, with a doctorate degree from Boston University, who led the civil rights movement in the late 1950s and early 1960s and was awarded the Nobel Peace Prize in 1964 for his model of nonviolent resistance as a means to achieve racial equality.

It astounds many young Americans to realize that, well into the 1960s, there were many parts of this country where blacks and whites were kept apart, not only by custom or

MARTIN LUTHER KING, Jr.
1929-1968

Martin Luther King's challenges to segregation and racial discrimination in the 1950s and 1960s helped convince many white Americans to support the cause of civil rights in the United States. After his assassination in 1968, King became a symbol of protest in the struggle for racial justice.

preference, but by laws. Blacks were not allowed to attend the same schools, visit the same hospitals, or apply for the same jobs that white Americans were. There were black restrooms and benches, black sections in movie theaters, black seats on the bus. There were clubs and organizations to which blacks were not allowed to belong. There were neighborhoods in which it was not safe for a black man to travel.

The roots of racial prejudice, and the reasons it stirs such strong and often violent emotions in many, are beyond the scope of this text. The point to be made here is that there was considerable anger and resistance, particularly in the South, but also in many other parts of the country as well, to the civil rights movement. At first, many groups felt it absolutely necessary to resist any change in

what they saw as a delicate truce between the races. These were not only working-class whites, but many white intellectuals and political leaders of the time. Many simply believed that blacks and whites could not mix or get along together without animosity and a threat of violence. Some of the more radical of these groups, such as the Ku Klux Klan, were willing to use violent means in order to resist this growing movement for social change.

The civil rights movement looked to do more than change people's attitudes. It sought to change the law, to force change upon society by desegregating city buses and integrating public school systems, even if this meant busing black or white students to schools they had not previously attended in order to achieve a better racial mix. In theory, blacks already had "separate but equal" institutions and rights.

However, in practice, the system of segregation perpetuated deep social and economic injustices. Unless something was done to prohibit discriminatory practices in hiring, voting requirements, or in access to services, there was little hope that true equality would ever be achieved.

Not all blacks who participated in the civil rights movement were advocates of nonviolence. Dr. King, however, was particularly strong in his beliefs in this regard. He knew that many white people were afraid of blacks and realized that only by demonstrating that black people were caring Christians, very much like white Americans saw themselves, could these barriers of fear be broken down in the majority of American citizens, making true change possible. The tactics employed involved orderly marches and demonstrations, chanting, distribution of literature, and speeches. Gradually, a significant number of young, white Americans became sympathetic to the cause and began to participate in the movement. This eventually led some politicians, such as the Kennedys, to publicly advocate the first meaningful federal civil rights laws.

King lived a difficult life in very difficult times. His leadership was challenged by more militant blacks. Some white people sought to intimidate him, or worse. There were bombings in churches, attacks against individual blacks, and counterdemonstrations, particularly at events such as the forced integration of public schools for the first time. Through it all, Dr. King maintained his composure, his religious convictions, and his optimism and sense of purpose. He understood that all white people should not be condemned for the actions of a few, and asked that white people view blacks in the same way.

Dr. King was assassinated on April 4, 1968, in Memphis, Tennessee. Although his assassination sparked incidents of violence, the values he devoted his life to fostering proved to be stronger, and the movement, though splintered, continued as many of his followers took up the cause. They preserved his nonviolent approach and gradually achieved one success after another in making changes on both state and federal levels.

Many would say that the civil rights movement is an ongoing struggle and that, even today, there is still much work to be done. Clearly, however, the country would not have grown and matured nearly as well as it did, nor would such sweeping changes have been made with such relatively little violence, had it not been for Martin Luther King's efforts.

ALBERT EINSTEIN

It may surprise some to see Albert Einstein mentioned as a famous American. This German-born physicist was already world-renowned for his scientific discoveries, and had indeed won the Nobel Prize for physics in 1921, long before he ever immigrated to the United States. During the final period of his life, however, he not only lived and taught in America, but he also made some important contributions to our history in helping to develop the atomic bomb.

It is important for everyone to realize that there are two basic ways to become an

American. The first is to be born here. The second is to immigrate to this country and become a naturalized American citizen. This is what Einstein did, and once he received his citizenship, he became an American equal to any other and thus equally worthy of mention in any chronicle of American history.

Einstein is regarded as one of the most brilliant and innovative minds of all time. Indeed, his name is sometimes synonymous with the notion of "genius." His theories of relativity drastically revolutionized the field of physics and made possible a great many scientific discoveries, of which nuclear weapons was only a small and almost coincidental part.

Some people mistakenly believe that Einstein worked directly to develop the atomic bomb. This is not true. Einstein was instrumental in persuading the United States of the possibility and importance of developing such a weapon. In order to understand how and why he did this, one needs to look into the tragic phase of his life, when he had to flee Nazi Germany and its intolerance in the 1930s. Einstein was perceptive not only in the realm of science but also in the theater of politics and international events.

Well before World War II, Einstein was very quick to realize that Adolf Hitler posed a major threat, not only to German Jews such as himself, but to the world as a whole. In 1933, Einstein renounced his German citizenship and left the country, warning that the Nazis were about to plunge the world into another war. It would be many years before his warnings were taken seriously, but his vocal

ALBERT EINSTEIN
1879-1955

German-born physicist and Nobel laureate, best known as the creator of the special and general theories of relativity and for his bold hypothesis concerning the particle nature of light. He is perhaps the most well-known scientist of the twentieth century.

opposition put his life in danger. He went to England, and, soon after, settled in the United States. He took up residence at the Institute for Advanced Studies in Princeton, New Jersey, which became the focal point for his later research that aimed to unify the laws of physics.

Although most of Einstein's major scientific contributions were made before he immigrated to our country, throughout his life he remained so well respected among his colleagues that he found himself in a position of influence. When he learned that the Germans had succeeded in splitting the atom in 1939, he became one of many world scientists who came to believe that the development of the atomic bomb was not only possible, but imminent. He wrote an important letter to Franklin Roosevelt urging the United States to initiate its own atomic bomb research, a recommendation which led to the beginning of the Manhattan Project.

Einstein did not work at Los Alamos, where America's nuclear fission bomb was developed. However, it is probable that the project would never have been carried out were it not for his insistence and that of other scientists. At the time, most American politicians saw the idea of an atomic bomb as little more than science fiction. It is amazing to think now that a weapon that has had such an important role in modern history, both for its use and the threat of its use, was all but ignored until it was almost too late. There is little doubt that if the Germans had been the first to complete the development of the bomb, they would have used it, and the outcome of the Second World War would have been very different.

Einstein was a pacifist by nature, but world events caused him to believe in the need to act with force to repel a great evil that could not be stopped through peaceful negotiation. Ironically, Einstein's life, despite the great moments of discovery and triumph, was an often sad tale. Many tragic personal events left Einstein a lonely and troubled man. However, he mustered self-discipline and perseverance and remained active in one area or another right up to his death at Princeton in 1955. The vast majority of his life was devoted both to scientific and pacifist causes. The tragic events of World War II caught him, like most other Americans and other people in the world, in a whirlwind that was not of his making, but to which he made a conscientious and dedicated response.

One of Einstein's most enduring achievements was his attempt to reconcile science and religion. Einstein was not an atheist, like many other scientists of his day, and he continually challenged scientists not to be narrow-minded in their pursuit of scientific evidence, but to continue to assess it philosophically in light of larger truths and values. Although it would be inaccurate to characterize Einstein as belonging to any particular traditional religious group, — he was much more of a free thinker — he continued to maintain an interest in his Jewish ancestry. It should also be noted that, after the war, he joined a group of scientists who sought to prevent any future use of the atomic bomb, although many of their specific plans and ideas did not come to pass. He remained an example of integrity and a willingness to explore the truth, however difficult or painful it might be.

SUSAN B. ANTHONY

It is regrettable that there are many Americans today who have never heard of Susan B. Anthony, and perhaps almost as regrettable that those who do know of her, think of her exclusively as a crusader for the right of American women to vote. While surely this was one of her most important causes, when Susan Anthony died at the age of 86 in 1906, the 19th Amendment to the U.S. Constitution, which would finally give women the right to vote, was still fourteen years in the future. It is astonishing, and some would say shameful, that an entire lifetime of dedicated work was not quite long enough to achieve an objective that we take for granted today: the political equality of women in our society. Nonetheless, the civic rights of women were as strenuously opposed by male Americans for decades as was the extension of civil rights to blacks. Indeed, black males gained voting rights over fifty years before American women did.

The fight for women's rights was not the first cause that came to Susan Anthony. Born to a Quaker family, she grew up in an atmosphere where moral values were highly stressed. This induced her to care about disadvantaged people of any type in society and propelled her to become active in the anti-slavery movement in the 1850s. After the Civil War was won, and after civil and political rights began to be given to male blacks, Anthony became especially vocal in her advocacy of women's rights. She used the rights given to blacks as an example of the rights she sought for all women, leading a vigorous campaign for the right to vote (called "suffrage") that occupied most of the rest of her life.

She lectured across the U.S. and in Europe. She organized several associations and compiled and published important books chronicling the history of the suffrage movement. In 1872, she led a nonviolent protest march in which women went to the

SUSAN B. ANTHONY
1820-1906

A liberal Quaker and dedicated radical reformer, Anthony opposed the use of liquor and advocated the immediate end of slavery. From 1848 to 1853 she took part in the temperance movement and from 1856 to 1861 worked for the American Anti-Slavery Society, organizing meetings and frequently giving lectures. In 1863, during the American Civil War, she founded the Women's Loyal League to fight for emancipation of the slaves. After the end of Reconstruction she protested the violence afflicted on blacks and was one of the few to urge full participation of blacks in the women's suffrage movement.

polls in Rochester and demanded the right to vote. For this, she was arrested and convicted, but she refused to pay the fine assigned by the court. Undaunted, she continued her struggle, despite the fact that at many points it must surely have seemed like victory would never be achieved. She inspired a great many other women and men who eventually took up the cause and continued it after her death, prompting many individual states one by one to extend the right to vote to women and leading to ultimate victory when the 19th Amendment was passed in 1920.

Since Susan B. Anthony, the women's rights movement has continued to grow. Many other American women, along with women in other parts of the world, have become prominent in their work for causes such as fair employment practices, equal pay for work of equal value, and an end to a wide range of economic, social, and political practices that continue to inhibit true gender equality.

Anthony's struggle on behalf of American women can easily be compared to Dr. King's struggle on behalf of American blacks. Her protests were nonviolent, and she persevered in the face of ridicule and opposition by forces which seemed far more powerful — yet, in the end, she prevailed. Although the steps she took were perhaps only the first few tiny steps in the long struggle for women's equality in American society, she played an instrumental role in building a lasting women's rights movement. As with the issue of the rights of black Americans, there are many who feel that the work is not yet done, though the progress that has been made over the last hundred years is certainly worthy of note.

Like Dr. King and Albert Einstein, Susan B. Anthony's work extended beyond the boundaries of our nation and influenced the development of the modern world as a whole. Although many consider the treatment of women in our early history to be shameful, there are certainly other parts of the world where it

has been much more so and where the atmosphere continues to be repressive to this day. The women's rights movement largely began in America and England, but it has become one of the most significant international causes, as well as one which has stimulated the greatest degree of social change in our modern society.

CESAR CHAVEZ

Up to now, we have seen that several groups within our nation had to struggle for equality to achieve the rights, freedoms, and standards of fair treatment and justice they enjoy today. The struggles that have shaped our nation have not only been among races or even between the sexes, but also, to a large extent, between the classes. Working-class Americans of any race have also struggled to achieve rights and enjoy protection and fair treatment in our society. This is the struggle of organized labor, and it is an important part of American history.

Cesar Chavez is a relatively small part of the struggle of the U.S. labor movement. We have chosen to include him here because he is also a hero of Hispanics and Latinos in America and his efforts at organizing the labor movement in California were made even more difficult by discrimination against Mexican Americans.

Chavez was not an immigrant; he was born in Arizona in 1927 to parents of Mexican descent. From an early age, like most Mexican Americans in that part of the world in those times, he worked in the agricultural fields. Shortly after

CESAR CHAVEZ
1927-1993

In 1968 Cesar Chavez gained much attention as leader of a nationwide boycott of California table grapes in a drive to achieve labor contracts. The struggle continued until the 1970s.

World War II, he served in the U.S. Navy. It was after his return from the service that he became active in the American labor movement. He had served his country and put his life on the line like any other American serviceman, and he felt entitled to be treated like any other citizen. He became concerned about the plight of American workers in general, and of Mexican Americans in particular. Like so many other idealists, he became convinced that he himself had to help improve the situation.

Between 1945 and 1965, he gradually worked his way up within the American labor movement. He first joined the National Agricultural Workers Union and then the Community Service Organization (CSO). However, although he rose to become the General Director of the CSO, he resigned in 1962 because the organization refused to recognize farm workers. He went on to found the National Farm Workers Association.

Chavez rose to national and international fame when he organized a strike and boycott against grape growers in California in 1965. It is important to understand that, at the time, the conditions of farm workers in that part of the world were deplorable. The workers had few rights, were paid a meager wage and were subjected to abuse and exposure to dangerous pesticides, which were sometimes sprayed onto the fields while they worked.

It was only as the American public became educated about the condition of the farm workers that pressure was placed on the growers to change their ways and negotiate with Chavez and his organization. The grape boycott was so effective that, by 1970, Chavez's organization had signed contracts with many of the major grape growers. From there, he turned his sights to the plight of lettuce growers in California, although that campaign was somewhat less successful. In 1973, Chavez became president of the United Farm Workers of America and continued his active leadership in the union movement into the 1980s.

In viewing the life and work of Cesar Chavez, it is important to note that his contributions stood alongside those of many dozens of other labor leaders in the country who worked in the factories, coal mines, shipyards, and in virtually every other element of American industry. As with the struggle for civil rights or equality of the sexes, there was initially considerable and powerful opposition to the union movement. In its early days, the movement was equated with communism and its leaders disparaged as traitors to America. Along the way, there was considerable animosity and hostility. Although most labor leaders organized legal strikes and peaceful demonstrations, violent tactics were occasionally used on the part of some business owners in order to break up and suppress the movement. As with any other meaningful form of change in America, it took a long and persistent struggle, gradually educating the American public and affecting public opinion, before politicians took up the cause. Today, American labor law is much more effective in protecting workers' rights, and Cesar Chavez is one of many dedicated Americans that the American worker has to thank.

SITTING BULL

By now, it has become clear that virtually every group in American society had to struggle, at one time or another, to achieve its place in our nation. Even white males of European decent, the group against whom most other groups have had to struggle at one time or another, faced their initial struggle for freedom in the Revolutionary War. Since then, many other groups have found that, while America was conceived with the highest ideals, it has often taken a difficult struggle to have those ideals applied fairly to a given group or in a given situation.

Americans value and admire success, but it would be unfair to dismiss all of those who struggled in our nation but who ultimately failed to achieve what they set out to do. They have nonetheless contributed, even in personal defeat, by inspiring others around them to take up the cause.

Throughout much of his life, the Sioux chief Sitting Bull was feared and despised by white Americans. Most failed to understand the details of his personal struggle and the very uninspirational actions of U.S. government officials that led not only to most of the conflict, but to the great personal tragedy that surrounds much of Sitting Bull's life.

Sitting Bull was born around 1831 in the Hunkpapa Sioux tribe. He became part of the "Strong Heart" warrior society, and his ability and willingness to wage war is certainly an undeniable part of Sitting Bull's personal history. His first scrimmage with white soldiers occurred in 1863, and, thereafter, much of the rest of his life was dedicated to military campaigns. Although ultimately, like almost all of the other Native American warriors, he was defeated, he was also responsible for some of the most stunning victories in the Indian Wars. These include the famous Battle of the Rosebud, where he defeated General George Crook, and his even more famous victory over Lieutenant Colonel George Custer in the Battle of Little Bighorn in 1876. He put together a formidable force from the Sioux and Cheyenne nations.

Sitting Bull was well admired and respected by the Native peoples of America, not only for his military successes, but also as a loving

SITTING BULL
1831?-1890

In 1885 Sitting Bull was allowed to leave the reservation to tour with the Wild West show of Buffalo Bill. There is speculation that permission was given because the Native American police wanted Sitting Bull off the reservation to prevent him from creating problems. The tense situation among the Sioux was aggravated by followers of the Native American messiah Wovoka, who promised the defeat of the whites.

father of his people and a person devoutly religious in the native faith. Like many other great Americans, he was an intelligent, intense, and complex person with many interests, a great zeal and drive to succeed, and a rigorous self-discipline which emerged from his warrior traditions.

Because his military campaigns led to the deaths of many white Americans, many Americans refuse to grant Sitting Bull any status

of honor as a figure in American history. However, it is important to understand the provocations that led to these bloody conflicts. Sitting Bull understood that the native way of life was dependent on the freedom to use ancestral lands and, in particular, to hunt the buffalo that sustained the Native population. He watched as one treaty after another was violated and white men expropriated the resources found on native lands. When gold was discovered in the Black Hills in the 1870s, treaty provisions were ignored and several provocations resulted in Sitting Bull's increasing defiance of white authorities. Ironically, some of the pronouncements that were made by federal commissioners in those days would have been impossible to obey even if he had wanted to. For example, in 1876, all Sioux were ordered to settle on reservations by a specified date or they would automatically be seen as hostile to the United States. It would not have been possible for Sitting Bull to have moved his entire village the distance that was required in the bitter cold of winter by the specified time.

Ironically, it was Sitting Bull's greatest victories that ultimately made his defeat inevitable. After their embarrassing defeat at the Battle of Little Bighorn, U.S. troops became more determined to drive Sitting Bull into submission. At about this time, the buffalo on the plains were being killed so rapidly by whites that they were soon on the verge of extinction. Faced not only with military opposition, but also growing hunger and poverty, the Sioux gradually surrendered to the American troops. In 1877, Sitting Bull led the remainder of his followers north of the border into Canada. There, far from his native lands, he had difficultly feeding his people. Famine forced him to surrender and return to the United States in 1883.

The final years of his life were marked by humiliation and tragedy. In 1890, when rumors began to spread that an Indian messiah was about to come and defeat the whites, there was so much unrest among the Sioux that an order was made to arrest Sitting Bull as a precautionary measure. He was killed while some of his warriors tried to rescue him.

Sitting Bull's life is not a great American success story. However, all lives, whether or not they achieve their desired objectives, influence the lives of many other people, and Sitting Bull's influence was pervasive among the native peoples of America and beyond. Gradually, as his true story began to be told in the 1930s, the public began to view the events of Sitting Bull's life from a new perspective. There is still, to this day, a great deal of work to be done to atone for the unfair treatment of Native Americans and to settle the complex and pervasive problems that still plague them. However, as the American public continues to evolve its social conscience, there is hope that continued progress will be made in this area, as has taken place for so many other ethnic minorities within our society.

As late as the 1950s, most American children studied history books in grammar school that painted "the Indians" as ruthless, violent people who could not be trusted. Today, most informed Americans view Natives quite differently. Although there were atrocities on both sides during the periods of violent conflict, there is now a greater appreciation of Native culture, values, and beliefs.

Particularly as Americans become more aware of the environment and the urgent need to preserve and protect it, we look back upon the ancient traditions of the native peoples for inspiration and guidance. We can view the story of Sitting Bull and several other similar tragedies in American history as a warning of what can happen when greed or commercial exploitation become divorced from an ethical treatment of both our fellow man and of the natural environment.

JOHN GLENN

John Glenn, our final example of an important American, has led a long and diverse life that has enabled him to excel in several different fields in both public and private life. A product of the heartland of America, Glenn is viewed as a moderate Democrat and a religious, sincere, and well-liked man. He joined the U.S. Marine Corps in 1943 and then served as a fighter pilot in World War II and the Korean War. He then served as a test pilot and was selected to be among the very first American astronauts in the early days of the Mercury space program.

Glenn became the third American to be blasted off into space, and the first to successfully orbit the earth, in his Friendship 7 capsule in 1962. That accomplishment in itself would have guaranteed Glenn a permanent place in American history, but it was only the beginning of his many visible public achievements.

Thirty-six years later, in October of 1998, John Glenn was selected to become the world's oldest man in space and returned to his role as an astronaut aboard the space shuttle Discovery. In the intervening years, he led an active political life that had made him one of the most respected of all American politicians and even ran for president in 1984.

After leaving the space program for the first time in 1964, he spent a decade working in private industry before deciding on a political career. In 1974, he was elected a U.S. senator from Ohio and was reelected to three terms. In his twenty-four year career in Congress, ending in retirement in 1999, he became one of the most revered American political figures of the twentieth century. Honest and reliable, he was respected by members of both political parties. Throughout his career, he had many interests, but perhaps the one for which he will be most lastingly remembered was his contribution as a member of the Senate Special Committee on Aging.

John Glenn was seventy-seven when he served as a crew member on the Discovery. Given the intense physical demands of space travel, there were many who wondered if he could withstand the stress. Nonetheless, he came through with flying colors, and served as an inspiration for America's aging population. Glenn is proof that senior citizens can be leaders.

There is a certain irony in John Glenn's triumph as a model for fighting discrimination on the basis of age. Even as an original member of the Mercury program, he was older than the other astronauts. He was already forty when he made his historic flight in 1962. Afterwards, he expected to continue

JOHN GLENN
1921-

After his initial historic flight, Glenn returned to the U.S. as a national hero. His character and charm made him one of the most popular Mercury astronauts and made NASA reluctant to risk his life by sending him back into space. Frustrated by the government's refusal to allow him to fly in space again, Glenn retired from NASA and the Marine Corps in 1965. His many military and space program awards and honors include the Distinguished Flying Cross, which he was awarded five times, and the Air Medal with 18 clusters.

to be an astronaut in the Gemini and Apollo programs that followed, but found himself constantly passed over for younger candidates (in part because of an accident that damaged his inner ear). It was doubtless a great moment of personal vindication for him to find that the man who seemed a little too old to go into space in 1964 was still up for the task in 1998!

Perhaps equal to his accomplishments in the military, the space program, and Congress is the example of John Glenn's personal character. He has had a solid marriage to his wife, Annie, since 1943. He proved that politicians don't have to be ruthless to win elections. He proved that the adage "nice guys finish last" is not always the case. He proved that it is possible to spend a lifetime being loyal to moral, religious, and political values, not to mention hard work, courage, and dedication to this country.

On a few occasions, Glenn came close to losing his life. In one combat flight over Korea, his aircraft was hit with heavy anti-aircraft fire that ripped one bomb from the underside of his plane and punctured its skin with more than two hundred bullet and shrapnel holes. He barely managed to keep his plane from crashing. Even his historic 1962 space flight flirted with disaster. During reentry into the earth's atmosphere, a task which had been accomplished only twice before, there was a problem with the heat shield on his capsule and many of the NASA launch control personnel feared that he and his capsule would burn up before he managed to splash down in the ocean.

Even Glenn's long and successful political career did not come to him easily. When he tried for a Senate seat in 1970, he lost the Ohio Democratic nomination. However, he didn't give up, and four years later he won the primary and went on to be elected. Nothing was handed to him and nothing came easy in his life.

It is perhaps this aspect of the man which makes him the typical and perhaps prototypical American hero. America most treasures those who are "self-made" men and women, those who were not born into prosperity or favor, but who had to work their way up and overcome adversity and disappointment to achieve final success.

Of course, not everyone is able to triumph. The American dream sometimes fails. Not all of our pilots who go into combat dance through the bullets and return to talk about it. John Glenn's astronaut colleague, Virgil "Gus" Grissom, was killed in a flash fire while preparing for an Apollo mission in 1967. As much as we owe our nation and its achievements to our great heroes and those who have led us in victory, we owe an equal if not greater debt to a great many who have worked hard and struggled without fame or fortune, men and women who may not have achieved all of their objectives, or whose lives may have been cut short by personal tragedies. While we always look to heroes, perhaps the greatness of our nation lies in our respect for the common, hard-working American who does their job to the best of their ability, puts their life on the line when necessary, and keeps our country moving, growing, and competing in the world.

Chapter Six • Recap Quiz

1. Who won the Nobel Peace Prize in 1964?

2. What non-scientific interest or activity is Albert Einstein also remembered for, in addition to his scientific work?

3. Susan Anthony fought for the right of American women to vote, but died fourteen years before this right became the subject of a Constitutional amendment. In what year did she die?

4. What was the name of the famous battle in which Sitting Bull defeated Lieutenant Colonel George Custer?

5. What was the name of the space capsule in which John Glenn became the first man to orbit the earth?

★ ★ ★ ★ ★ ★ ★ ★ ★ ★

ANSWERS TO QUIZ SIX

1- Martin Luther King   2- pacifism   3- 1906

4- the Battle of Little Bighorn   5- Friendship 7

The following is an abbreviated listing of many famous and important events in American history, showing their dates and the order in which they occurred. It includes events discussed in this text, as well as others which were not mentioned here, but which you may wish to investigate through further reading and study.

B.C. 38,000 —	Paleo-Indians make first movement into North America via landbridge to Alaska (approximate date)
A.D. 1,000 —	Vikings become first Europeans to sail to any part of North America (Vinland) (approximate date)
1492 —	Columbus sails to America
1620 —	Pilgrims sail Mayflower to Plymouth, Mass.
1754 to 1763 —	French and Indian War; British take control of most of North America
1765 —	Stamp Act enrages colonists
1775 —	First battles of Revolutionary War fought
1776 —	Declaration of Independence
1781 —	Cornwallis surrenders at Yorktown to end Revolutionary War
1787 —	Constitutional Convention
1789 —	George Washington becomes president
1789 —	Bill of Rights
1797 —	John Adams becomes president

1801 —	Thomas Jefferson becomes president
1803 —	Louisiana Purchase: U.S. purchases large territory in the midwest, from France
1809 —	James Madison becomes president
1812 to 1815 —	War of 1812
1817 —	James Monroe becomes president
1823 —	Monroe Doctrine: U.S. declares opposition to European intervention in the Americas
1825 —	John Quincy Adams becomes president
1829 —	Andrew Jackson becomes president
1837 —	widespread economic depression
1846 —	Lincoln elected to Congress
1846 to 1848 —	Mexican-American War
1860 —	South Carolina secedes from the Union
1861 —	Abraham Lincoln becomes president
1861 to 1865 —	Civil War
1863 —	Emancipation Proclamation
1865 —	Lincoln assassinated
1865 —	Andrew Johnson becomes president
1869 —	U.S. Grant becomes president

1876 —	Sitting Bull wins Battle of Little Bighorn
1898 —	Spanish-American War
1901 —	President McKinley assassinated
1901 —	Theodore Roosevelt becomes president
1906 —	Susan B. Anthony dies
1913 —	Woodrow Wilson becomes president
1913 —	Federal income tax introduced by Constitutional amendment
1914 —	World War I starts in Europe
1917 to 1918 —	U.S. involvement in World War I
1920 —	U.S. women gain right to vote under 19th Amendment
1929 to 1941 —	Great Depression
1933 —	Franklin Roosevelt becomes president
1939 —	World War II begins in Europe
1941 to 1945 —	U.S. involvement in World War II
1945 —	Harry Truman becomes president
1950 to 1953 —	Korean War
1953 —	Dwight Eisenhower becomes president
1961 —	John Kennedy becomes president
1962 —	John Glenn becomes first man to orbit earth

1963 —	Kennedy assassinated
1963 —	Lyndon Johnson becomes president
1964 —	Civil Rights Act
1964 to 1973 —	U.S. involvement in Vietnam War
1965 —	Cesar Chavez launches California grape boycott
1968 —	Martin Luther King assassinated
1968 —	Robert Kennedy assassinated
1969 —	Richard Nixon becomes president
1969 —	First American astronauts walk on moon
1972 —	Strategic Arms Limitation Treaty signed with Soviet Union
1972 —	Nixon visits China
1973 —	Watergate hearings in Senate
1974 —	Nixon resigns
1974 —	Gerald Ford becomes president
1974 —	Ford pardons Nixon for Watergate
1975 —	South Vietnam defeated by communists, Vietnam reunited
1977 —	Jimmy Carter becomes president
1979 —	U.S. hostages taken in Iran
1981 —	Ronald Reagan becomes president

1982 —	Economic recession begins
1983 —	U.S. troops sent to Lebanon
1983 —	U.S. invades Grenada
1984 —	Reagan visits China
1985 —	Reagan meets Soviet leader Gorbachev
1987 —	Iran-Contra hearings
1987 —	Arms limitation treaty with Soviet Union
1989 —	George H. W. Bush becomes president
1989 —	U.S. invades Panama
1991 —	Gulf War against Iraq
1993 —	Bill Clinton becomes president
1997 —	Oklahoma bombing trial ends with conviction of Timothy McVeigh
1998 —	John Glenn returns to space
1999 —	Failed impeachment attempt against Clinton
1999 —	U.S.-led NATO action in Kosovo
2001 —	George W. Bush becomes president
2001 —	World Trade Center and Pentagon attacked
2001 —	War on Terrorism begins
2003 —	U.S. leads invasion of Iraq and removes Saddam Hussein from power

There are literally thousands of books about American history filling public and university libraries. The following titles, listed alphabetically by author, represent a small sample of suggestions for those who would like to pursue a further study of subjects covered in this text, and other topics not dealt with here.

Ackerman, Frank. Reaganomics. 1982.

Alexander, Charles C. Holding the Line: The Eisenhower Era. 1951-1962. 1975.

Alperovitz, Gar. Atomic Diplomacy: Hiroshima and Potsdam. 1985.

Atkinson, Rick. Crusade: The Untold Story of the Persian Gulf War. 1993.

Badger, Anthony. The New Deal: The Depression Years, 1933-1940. 1989.

Bailyn, Bernard. The Origins of American Politics. 1968.

Barlow, J. Jackson et al. The American Founding: Essays on the Formation of the Constitution. 1988.

Beal, Howard K. Theodore Roosevelt and the Rise of America to World Power. 1956.

Bernstein, Carl and Bob Woodward. All the President's Men. 1974.

Beschloss, Michael. The Crisis Years: Kennedy and Krushchev, 1961-1963. 1991.

Billington, Ray Allen. Westward Expansion: A History of the American Frontier. 1967.

Bloom, Jack. Class, Race, and the Civil Rights Movement. 1987.

Blum, John Morton. V Was for Victory: Politics and American Culture During World War II. 1976.

Bornet, Vaugh D. The Presidency of Lyndon B. Johnson. 1983.

Countryman, Edward. The American Revolution. 1985.

Crane, Verner W. <u>Benjamin Franklin and a Rising People.</u> 1954.

Cressy, David. <u>Coming Over: Migration and Communication Between England and New England in the Seventeenth Century.</u> 1987.

Donovan, Robert J. <u>Conflict and Crisis: The Presidency of Harry S. Truman, 1949-1953.</u> 1982.

Duffy, Michael. <u>Marching in Place: The Status Quo Presidency of George Bush.</u> 1992.

Dubois, Ellen. <u>Feminism and Suffrage.</u> 1978.

Fiedel, Stuart. <u>The Prehistory of the Americas.</u> 1987.

Freman, Jo. <u>The Politics of Women's Liberation.</u> 1975.

Garrow, David J. <u>Bearing the Cross: Martin Luther King Jr. and the Southern Christian Leadership Conference.</u> 1986.

Gibson, Charles. <u>Spain in America.</u> 1966.

Hartmann, Robert. <u>Palace Politics: An Inside Account of the Ford Years.</u> 1980.

Hickey, Donald R. <u>The War of 1812: A Forgotten Conflict.</u> 1989.

Hitchens, Christopher. <u>No One Left to Lie To: The Triangulations of William Jefferson Clinton.</u> 1999.

Hunter, James Davidson. <u>Culture Wars: The Struggle to Define America.</u> 1991.

Johannsen, Robert W. <u>To the Halls of Montezuma: The Mexican War in the American Imagination.</u> 1985.

Kaufman, Burton I. <u>The Presidency of James Earl Carter.</u> 1993.

Kehoe, Alice B. <u>North American Indians: A Comprehensive Account.</u> 1992.

Knock, Thomas J. <u>To End All Wars.</u> 1992 (World War I)

Kolchin, Peter. <u>American Slavery: 1619-1877.</u> 1993.

Kraditor, Aileen. <u>The Ideas of the Woman Suffrage Movement.</u> 1981.

LaFever, Walter. <u>America, Russia, and the Cold War, 1945-1980.</u> 1985.

Link, Arthur S. <u>Woodrow Wilson: Revolution, War, and Peace.</u> 1979.

Main, Jackson Turner. <u>The Social Structure of Revolutionary America.</u> 1965.

Maraniss, David. <u>First in His Class: A Biography of Bill Clinton.</u> 1995.

McDonald, Forrest. <u>The Presidency of George Washington.</u> 1974.

McDougall, Walter A. <u>The Heavens and the Earth: A Political History of the Space Age.</u> 1985.

McPherson, James. <u>Battle Cry of Freedom: The Civil War Era.</u> 1988.

Mintz, Steven and Susan Kellogg. <u>Domestic Revolutions: A Social History of American Family Life.</u> 1988.

Parmet, Herbert. <u>JFK: The Presidency of John F. Kennedy.</u> 1983.

Parmet, Herbert. <u>Richard Nixon and His America.</u> 1990.

Peterson, Merrill. <u>Thomas Jefferson and the New Nation.</u> 1970.

Prucha, Francis Paul. <u>American Indian Policy in Crisis.</u> 1976.

Rawley, James A. <u>The Transatlantic Slave Trade, A History.</u> 1981.

Roosevelt, Theodore. <u>The Rough Riders.</u> 1899.

Rutland, Robert A. <u>The Birth of the Bill of Rights.</u> 1955.

Santoli, Al. <u>New Americans: An Oral History.</u> 1988,

Schlesinger, Arthur M. <u>The Age of Roosevelt.</u> 1983.

Schroeder, John H. <u>Mr. Polk's War: American Opposition and Dissent, 1946-1848.</u> 1973.

Sitkoff, Harvard. <u>The Struggle for Black Equality.</u> 1981.

Trachtenberg, Alan. <u>The Incorporation of America: Culture and Society in the Gilded Age.</u> 1982.

Trask, David F. <u>The War with Spain in 1898.</u> 1981.

Vestal, Stanley. <u>Sitting Bull.</u> 1957.

Wills, Garry. <u>Reagan's America.</u> 1987.

Wilson, Douglas L. <u>Honor's Voice: The Transformation of Abraham Lincoln.</u> 1998.

Wertheimer, Barbara. <u>We Were There: The Story of Working Women in America.</u> 1977.

Woodward, Bob. <u>Veil: The Secret Wars of the CIA.</u> 1987.

Young, Marilyn B. <u>The Vietnam Wars, 1945-1990.</u> 1991.

NOTE:
A wide range of publications on specific topics and issues, some of them very concise, can be obtained from The American Historical Association. For more information on what is available they may be contacted at (202) 544-2422.

USEFUL WEB SITES

There are many websites which offer information about American history. Here are a couple of interesting ones to get you started...

www.thehistorynet.com — American and world history

www.whitehouse.gov — presidents and first ladies

www.civil-war.net — Civil War

www.ksc.nasa.gov — U.S. space program

IN CONGRESS, July 4, 1776.

Complete Text – Transcription

The unanimous Declaration of the thirteen united States of America,

When in the Course of human events, it becomes necessary for one people to dissolve the political bands which have connected them with another, and to assume among the powers of the earth, the separate and equal station to which the Laws of Nature and of Nature's God entitle them, a decent respect to the opinions of mankind requires that they should declare the causes which impel them to the separation.

We hold these truths to be self-evident, that all men are created equal, that they are endowed by their Creator with certain unalienable Rights, that among these are Life, Liberty and the pursuit of Happiness. — That to secure these rights, Governments are instituted among Men, deriving their just powers from the consent of the governed, — That whenever any Form of Government becomes destructive of these ends, it is the Right of the People to alter or to abolish it, and to institute new Government, laying its foundation on such principles and organizing its powers in such form, as to them shall seem most likely to effect their Safety and Happiness. Prudence, indeed, will dictate that Governments long established should not be changed for light and transient causes; and accordingly all experience hath shewn, that mankind are more disposed to suffer, while evils are sufferable, than to right themselves by abolishing the forms to which they are accustomed. But when a long train of abuses and usurpations, pursuing invariably the same Object evinces a design to reduce them under absolute Despotism, it is their right, it is their duty, to throw off such Government, and to provide new Guards for their future security. — Such has been the patient sufferance of these Colonies; and such is now the necessity which constrains them to alter their former Systems of Government. The history of the present King of Great Britain is a history of repeated injuries and usurpations, all having in direct object the establishment of an absolute Tyranny over these States. To prove this, let Facts be submitted to a candid world.

He has refused his Assent to Laws, the most wholesome and necessary for the public good.

He has forbidden his Governors to pass Laws of immediate and pressing importance, unless suspended in their operation till his Assent should be obtained; and when so suspended, he has utterly neglected to attend to them.

He has refused to pass other Laws for the accommodation of large districts of people, unless those people would relinquish the right of Representation in the Legislature, a right inestimable to them and formidable to tyrants only.

He has called together legislative bodies at places unusual, uncomfortable, and distant from the depository of their public Records, for the sole purpose of fatiguing them into compliance with his measures.

He has dissolved Representative Houses repeatedly, for opposing with manly firmness his invasions on the rights of the people.

He has refused for a long time, after such dissolutions, to cause others to be elected; whereby the Legislative powers, incapable of Annihilation, have returned to the People at large for their exercise; the State remaining in the mean time exposed to all the dangers of invasion from without, and convulsions within.

He has endeavoured to prevent the population of these States; for that purpose obstructing the Laws for Naturalization of Foreigners; refusing to pass others to encourage their migrations hither, and raising the conditions of new Appropriations of Lands.

He has obstructed the Administration of Justice, by refusing his Assent to Laws for establishing Judiciary powers.

He has made Judges dependent on his Will alone, for the tenure of their offices, and the amount and payment of their salaries.

He has erected a multitude of New Offices, and sent hither swarms of Officers to harrass our people, and eat out their substance.

He has kept among us, in times of peace, Standing Armies without the Consent of our legislatures.

He has affected to render the Military independent of and superior to the Civil power.

He has combined with others to subject us to a jurisdiction foreign to our constitution, and unacknowledged by our laws; giving his Assent to their Acts of pretended Legislation:

For Quartering large bodies of armed troops among us:

For protecting them, by a mock Trial, from punishment for any Murders which they should commit on the Inhabitants of these States:

For cutting off our Trade with all parts of the world:

For imposing Taxes on us without our Consent:

For depriving us, in many cases, of the benefits of Trial by Jury:

For transporting us beyond Seas to be tried for pretended offences:

For abolishing the free System of English Laws in a neighbouring Province, establishing therein an Arbitrary government, and enlarging its Boundaries so as to render it at once an example and fit instrument for introducing the same absolute rule into these Colonies:

For taking away our Charters, abolishing our most valuable Laws, and altering fundamentally the Forms of our Governments:

For suspending our own Legislatures, and declaring themselves invested with power to legislate for us in all cases whatsoever.

He has abdicated Government here, by declaring us out of his Protection and waging War against us.

He has plundered our seas, ravaged our Coasts, burnt our towns, and destroyed the lives of our people.

He is at this time transporting large Armies of foreign Mercenaries to compleat the works of death, desolation and tyranny, already begun with circumstances of Cruelty & perfidy scarcely paralleled in the most barbarous ages, and totally unworthy the Head of a civilized nation.

He has constrained our fellow Citizens taken Captive on the high Seas to bear Arms against their Country, to become the executioners of their friends and Brethren, or to fall themselves by their Hands.

He has excited domestic insurrections amongst us, and has endeavoured to bring on the inhabitants of our frontiers, the merciless Indian Savages, whose known rule of warfare, is an undistinguished destruction of all ages, sexes and conditions.

In every stage of these Oppressions We have Petitioned for Redress in the most humble terms: Our repeated Petitions have been answered only by repeated injury. A Prince whose character is thus marked by every act which may define a Tyrant, is unfit to be the ruler of a free people.

Nor have We been wanting in attentions to our Brittish brethren. We have warned them from time to time of attempts by their legislature to extend an unwarrantable jurisdiction over us. We have reminded them of the circumstances of our emigration and settlement here. We have appealed to their native justice and magnanimity, and we have conjured them by the ties of our common kindred to disavow these usurpations, which, would inevitably interrupt our connections and correspondence. They too have been deaf to the voice of justice and of consanguinity. We must, therefore, acquiesce in the necessity, which denounces our Separation, and hold them, as we hold the rest of mankind, Enemies in War, in Peace Friends.

We, therefore, the Representatives of the united States of America, in General Congress, Assembled, appealing to the Supreme Judge of the world for the rectitude of our intentions, do, in the Name, and by Authority of the good People of these Colonies, solemnly publish and declare, That these United Colonies are, and of Right ought to be Free and Independent States; that they are Absolved from all Allegiance to the British Crown, and that all political connection between them and the State of Great Britain, is and ought to be totally dissolved; and that as Free and Independent States, they have full Power to levy War, conclude Peace, contract Alliances, establish Commerce, and to do all other Acts and Things which Independent States may of right do. And for the support of this Declaration, with a firm reliance on the protection of divine Providence, we mutually pledge to each other our Lives, our Fortunes and our sacred Honor.

Complete Text – Transcription

Constitution of the United States of America

We the People of the United States, in Order to form a more perfect Union, establish Justice, insure domestic Tranquility, provide for the common defense, promote the general Welfare, and secure the Blessings of Liberty to ourselves and our Posterity, do ordain and establish this Constitution for the United States of America.

Section. 1.
All legislative Powers herein granted shall be vested in a Congress of the United States, which shall consist of a Senate and House of Representatives.

Section. 2.
The House of Representatives shall be composed of Members chosen every second Year by the People of the several States, and the Electors in each State shall have the Qualifications requisite for Electors of the most numerous Branch of the State Legislature.

No Person shall be a Representative who shall not have attained to the Age of twenty five Years, and been seven Years a Citizen of the United States, and who shall not, when elected, be an Inhabitant of that State in which he shall be chosen.

Representatives and direct Taxes shall be apportioned among the several States which may be included within this Union, according to their respective Numbers, which shall be determined by adding to the whole Number of free Persons, including those bound to Service for a Term of Years, and excluding Indians not taxed, three fifths of all other Persons. The actual Enumeration shall be made within three Years after the first Meeting of the Congress of the United States, and within every subsequent Term of ten Years, in such Manner as they shall by Law direct. The Number of Representatives shall not exceed one for every thirty Thousand, but each State shall have at Least one Representative; and until such enumeration shall be made, the State of New Hampshire shall be entitled to chuse three, Massachusetts eight, Rhode-Island and Providence Plantations one, Connecticut five, New-York six, New Jersey four, Pennsylvania eight, Delaware one, Maryland six, Virginia ten, North Carolina five, South Carolina five, and Georgia three.

When vacancies happen in the Representation from any State, the Executive Authority thereof shall issue Writs of Election to fill such Vacancies.

The House of Representatives shall chuse their Speaker and other Officers; and shall have the sole Power of Impeachment.

Section. 3.

The Senate of the United States shall be composed of two Senators from each State, chosen by the Legislature thereof for six Years; and each Senator shall have one Vote.

Immediately after they shall be assembled in Consequence of the first Election, they shall be divided as equally as may be into three Classes. The Seats of the Senators of the first Class shall be vacated at the Expiration of the second Year, of the second Class at the Expiration of the fourth Year, and of the third Class at the Expiration of the sixth Year, so that one third may be chosen every second Year; and if Vacancies happen by Resignation, or otherwise, during the Recess of the Legislature of any State, the Executive thereof may make temporary Appointments until the next Meeting of the Legislature, which shall then fill such Vacancies.

No Person shall be a Senator who shall not have attained to the Age of thirty Years, and been nine Years a Citizen of the United States, and who shall not, when elected, be an Inhabitant of that State for which he shall be chosen.

The Vice President of the United States shall be President of the Senate, but shall have no Vote, unless they be equally divided.

The Senate shall chuse their other Officers, and also a President pro tempore, in the Absence of the Vice President, or when he shall exercise the Office of President of the United States.

The Senate shall have the sole Power to try all Impeachments. When sitting for that Purpose, they shall be on Oath or Affirmation. When the President of the United States is tried, the Chief Justice shall preside: And no Person shall be convicted without the Concurrence of two thirds of the Members present.

Judgment in Cases of Impeachment shall not extend further than to removal from Office, and disqualification to hold and enjoy any Office of honor, Trust or Profit under the United States: but the Party convicted shall nevertheless be liable and subject to Indictment, Trial, Judgment and Punishment, according to Law.

Section. 4.

The Times, Places and Manner of holding Elections for Senators and Representatives, shall be prescribed in each State by the Legislature thereof; but the Congress may at any time by Law make or alter such Regulations, except as to the Places of chusing Senators.

The Congress shall assemble at least once in every Year, and such Meeting shall be on the first Monday in December, unless they shall by Law appoint a different Day.

Section. 5.

Each House shall be the Judge of the Elections, Returns and Qualifications of its own Members, and a Majority of each shall constitute a Quorum to do Business; but a smaller Number may adjourn from day to day, and may be authorized to compel the Attendance of absent Members, in such Manner, and under such Penalties as each House may provide.

Each House may determine the Rules of its Proceedings, punish its Members for disorderly Behaviour, and, with the Concurrence of two thirds, expel a Member.

Each House shall keep a Journal of its Proceedings, and from time to time publish the same, excepting such Parts as may in their Judgment require Secrecy; and the Yeas and Nays of the Members of either House on any question shall, at the Desire of one fifth of those Present, be entered on the Journal.

Neither House, during the Session of Congress, shall, without the Consent of the other, adjourn for more than three days, nor to any other Place than that in which the two Houses shall be sitting.

Section. 6.

The Senators and Representatives shall receive a Compensation for their Services, to be ascertained by Law, and paid out of the Treasury of the United States. They shall in all Cases, except Treason, Felony and Breach of the Peace, be privileged from Arrest during their Attendance at the Session of their respective Houses, and in going to and returning from the same; and for any Speech or Debate in either House, they shall not be questioned in any other Place.

No Senator or Representative shall, during the Time for which he was elected, be appointed to any civil Office under the Authority of the United States, which shall have been created, or the Emoluments whereof shall have been encreased during such time; and no Person holding any Office under the United States, shall be a Member of either House during his Continuance in Office.

Section. 7.

All Bills for raising Revenue shall originate in the House of Representatives; but the Senate may propose or concur with Amendments as on other Bills.

Every Bill which shall have passed the House of Representatives and the Senate, shall, before it become a Law, be presented to the President of the United States: If he approve he shall sign it, but if not he shall return it, with his Objections to that House in which it shall have originated, who shall enter the Objections at large on their Journal, and proceed to reconsider it. If after such Reconsideration two thirds of that House shall agree to pass the Bill, it shall be sent, together with the Objections, to the other House, by which it shall likewise be reconsidered, and if approved by two thirds of that House, it shall become a Law. But in all such Cases the Votes of both Houses shall be determined by yeas and Nays, and the Names of the Persons voting for and against the Bill shall be entered on the Journal of each House respectively. If any Bill shall not be returned by the President within ten Days (Sundays excepted) after it shall have been presented to him, the Same shall be a Law, in like Manner as if he had signed it, unless the Congress by their Adjournment prevent its Return, in which Case it shall not be a Law.

Every Order, Resolution, or Vote to which the Concurrence of the Senate and House of Representatives may be necessary (except on a question of Adjournment) shall be presented to the President of the United States; and before the Same shall take Effect, shall be approved by him, or being disapproved by him, shall be repassed by two thirds of the Senate and House of Representatives, according to the Rules and Limitations prescribed in the Case of a Bill.

Section. 8.
The Congress shall have Power To lay and collect Taxes, Duties, Imposts and Excises, to pay the Debts and provide for the common Defence and general Welfare of the United States; but all Duties, Imposts and Excises shall be uniform throughout the United States;

To borrow Money on the credit of the United States;

To regulate Commerce with foreign Nations, and among the several States, and with the Indian Tribes;

To establish an uniform Rule of Naturalization, and uniform Laws on the subject of Bankruptcies throughout the United States;

To coin Money, regulate the Value thereof, and of foreign Coin, and fix the Standard of Weights and Measures;

To provide for the Punishment of counterfeiting the Securities and current Coin of the United States;

To establish Post Offices and post Roads;

To promote the Progress of Science and useful Arts, by securing for limited Times to Authors and Inventors the exclusive Right to their respective Writings and Discoveries;

To constitute Tribunals inferior to the supreme Court;

To define and punish Piracies and Felonies committed on the high Seas, and Offences against the Law of Nations;

To declare War, grant Letters of Marque and Reprisal, and make Rules concerning Captures on Land and Water;

To raise and support Armies, but no Appropriation of Money to that Use shall be for a longer Term than two Years;

To provide and maintain a Navy;

To make Rules for the Government and Regulation of the land and naval Forces;

To provide for calling forth the Militia to execute the Laws of the Union, suppress Insurrections and repel Invasions;

To provide for organizing, arming, and disciplining, the Militia, and for governing such Part of them as may be employed in the Service of the United States, reserving to the States respectively, the Appointment of the Officers, and the Authority of training the Militia according to the discipline prescribed by Congress;

To exercise exclusive Legislation in all Cases whatsoever, over such District (not exceeding ten Miles square) as may, by Cession of particular States, and the Acceptance of Congress, become the Seat of the Government of the United States, and to exercise like Authority over all Places purchased by the Consent of the Legislature of the State in which the Same shall be, for the Erection of Forts, Magazines, Arsenals, dock-Yards, and other needful Buildings;—And

To make all Laws which shall be necessary and proper for carrying into Execution the foregoing Powers, and all other Powers vested by this Constitution in the Government of the United States, or in any Department or Officer thereof.

Section. 9.

The Migration or Importation of such Persons as any of the States now existing shall think proper to admit, shall not be prohibited by the Congress prior to the Year one thousand eight hundred and eight, but a Tax or duty may be imposed on such Importation, not exceeding ten dollars for each Person.

The Privilege of the Writ of Habeas Corpus shall not be suspended, unless when in Cases of Rebellion or Invasion the public Safety may require it.

No Bill of Attainder or ex post facto Law shall be passed.

No Capitation, or other direct, Tax shall be laid, unless in Proportion to the Census or enumeration herein before directed to be taken.

No Tax or Duty shall be laid on Articles exported from any State.

No Preference shall be given by any Regulation of Commerce or Revenue to the Ports of one State over those of another; nor shall Vessels bound to, or from, one State, be obliged to enter, clear, or pay Duties in another.

No Money shall be drawn from the Treasury, but in Consequence of Appropriations made by Law; and a regular Statement and Account of the Receipts and Expenditures of all public Money shall be published from time to time.

No Title of Nobility shall be granted by the United States: And no Person holding any Office of Profit or Trust under them, shall, without the Consent of the Congress, accept of any present, Emolument, Office, or Title, of any kind whatever, from any King, Prince, or foreign State.

Section. 10.
No State shall enter into any Treaty, Alliance, or Confederation; grant Letters of Marque and Reprisal; coin Money; emit Bills of Credit; make any Thing but gold and silver Coin a Tender in Payment of Debts; pass any Bill of Attainder, ex post facto Law, or Law impairing the Obligation of Contracts, or grant any Title of Nobility.

No State shall, without the Consent of the Congress, lay any Imposts or Duties on Imports or Exports, except what may be absolutely necessary for executing it's inspection Laws: and the net Produce of all Duties and Imposts, laid by any State on Imports or Exports, shall be for the Use of the Treasury of the United States; and all such Laws shall be subject to the Revision and Controul of the Congress.

No State shall, without the Consent of Congress, lay any Duty of Tonnage, keep Troops, or Ships of War in time of Peace, enter into any Agreement or Compact with another State, or with a foreign Power, or engage in War, unless actually invaded, or in such imminent Danger as will not admit of delay.

Article. II.

Section. 1.
The executive Power shall be vested in a President of the United States of America. He shall hold his Office during the Term of four Years, and, together with the Vice President, chosen for the same Term, be elected, as follows:

Each State shall appoint, in such Manner as the Legislature thereof may direct, a Number of Electors, equal to the whole Number of Senators and Representatives to which the State may be entitled in the Congress: but no Senator or Representative, or Person holding an Office of Trust or Profit under the United States, shall be appointed an Elector.

The Electors shall meet in their respective States, and vote by Ballot for two Persons, of whom one at least shall not be an Inhabitant of the same State with themselves. And they shall make a List of all the Persons voted for, and of the Number of Votes for each; which List they shall sign and certify, and transmit sealed to the Seat of the Government of the United States, directed to the President of the Senate. The President of the Senate shall, in the Presence of the Senate and House of Representatives, open all the Certificates, and the Votes shall then be counted. The Person having the greatest Number of Votes shall be the President, if such Number be a Majority of the whole Number of Electors appointed; and if there be more than one who have such Majority, and have an equal Number of Votes, then the House of Representatives shall immediately chuse by Ballot one of them for President; and if no Person have a Majority, then from the five highest on the List the said House shall in like Manner chuse the President. But in chusing the President, the Votes shall be taken by States, the Representation from each State having one Vote; A quorum for this purpose shall consist of a Member or Members from two thirds of the States, and a Majority of all the States shall be necessary to a Choice. In every Case, after the Choice of the President, the Person having the greatest Number of Votes of the Electors shall be the Vice President. But if there should remain two or more who have equal Votes, the Senate shall chuse from them by Ballot the Vice President.

The Congress may determine the Time of chusing the Electors, and the Day on which they shall give their Votes; which Day shall be the same throughout the United States.

No Person except a natural born Citizen, or a Citizen of the United States, at the time of the Adoption of this Constitution, shall be eligible to the Office of President; neither shall any Person be eligible to that Office who shall not have attained to the Age of thirty five Years, and been fourteen Years a Resident within the United States.

In Case of the Removal of the President from Office, or of his Death, Resignation, or Inability to discharge the Powers and Duties of the said Office, the Same shall devolve on the Vice President, and the Congress may by Law provide for the Case of Removal, Death, Resignation or Inability, both of the President and Vice President, declaring what Officer shall then act as President, and such Officer shall act accordingly, until the Disability be removed, or a President shall be elected.

The President shall, at stated Times, receive for his Services, a Compensation, which shall neither be increased nor diminished during the Period for which he shall have been elected, and he shall not receive within that Period any other Emolument from the United States, or any of them.

Before he enter on the Execution of his Office, he shall take the following Oath or Affirmation:— "I do solemnly swear (or affirm) that I will faithfully execute the Office of President of the United States, and will to the best of my Ability, preserve, protect and defend the Constitution of the United States."

Section. 2.

The President shall be Commander in Chief of the Army and Navy of the United States, and of the Militia of the several States, when called into the actual Service of the United States; he may require the Opinion, in writing, of the principal Officer in each of the executive Departments, upon any Subject relating to the Duties of their respective Offices, and he shall have Power to grant Reprieves and Pardons for Offences against the United States, except in Cases of Impeachment.

He shall have Power, by and with the Advice and Consent of the Senate, to make Treaties, provided two thirds of the Senators present concur; and he shall nominate, and by and with the Advice and Consent of the Senate, shall appoint Ambassadors, other public Ministers and Consuls, Judges of the supreme Court, and all other Officers of the United States, whose Appointments are not herein otherwise provided for, and which shall be established by Law: but the Congress may by Law vest the Appointment of such inferior Officers, as they think proper, in the President alone, in the Courts of Law, or in the Heads of Departments.

The President shall have Power to fill up all Vacancies that may happen during the Recess of the Senate, by granting Commissions which shall expire at the End of their next Session.

Section. 3.

He shall from time to time give to the Congress Information of the State of the Union, and recommend to their Consideration such Measures as he shall judge necessary and expedient; he may, on extraordinary Occasions, convene both Houses, or either of them, and in Case of Disagreement between them, with Respect to the Time of Adjournment, he may adjourn them to such Time as he shall think proper; he shall receive Ambassadors and other public Ministers; he shall take Care that the Laws be faithfully executed, and shall Commission all the Officers of the United States.

Section. 4.

The President, Vice President and all civil Officers of the United States, shall be removed from Office on Impeachment for, and Conviction of, Treason, Bribery, or other high Crimes and Misdemeanors.

Article III.

Section. 1.

The judicial Power of the United States shall be vested in one supreme Court, and in such inferior Courts as the Congress may from time to time ordain and establish. The Judges, both of the supreme and inferior Courts, shall hold their Offices during good Behaviour, and shall, at stated Times, receive for their Services a Compensation, which shall not be diminished during their Continuance in Office.

Section. 2.

The judicial Power shall extend to all Cases, in Law and Equity, arising under this Constitution, the Laws of the United States, and Treaties made, or which shall be made, under their Authority;—to all Cases affecting Ambassadors, other public Ministers and Consuls;—to all Cases of admiralty and maritime Jurisdiction;—to Controversies to which the United States shall be a Party;—to Controversies between two or more States;— between a State and Citizens of another State;— between Citizens of different States;—between Citizens of the same State claiming Lands under Grants of different States, and between a State, or the Citizens thereof, and foreign States, Citizens or Subjects.

In all Cases affecting Ambassadors, other public Ministers and Consuls, and those in which a State shall be Party, the supreme Court shall have original Jurisdiction. In all the other Cases before mentioned, the supreme Court shall have appellate Jurisdiction, both as to Law and Fact, with such Exceptions, and under such Regulations as the Congress shall make.

The Trial of all Crimes, except in Cases of Impeachment, shall be by Jury; and such Trial shall be held in the State where the said Crimes shall have been committed; but when not committed within any State, the Trial shall be at such Place or Places as the Congress may by Law have directed.

Section. 3.

Treason against the United States, shall consist only in levying War against them, or in adhering to their Enemies, giving them Aid and Comfort. No Person shall be convicted of Treason unless on the Testimony of two Witnesses to the same overt Act, or on Confession in open Court.

The Congress shall have Power to declare the Punishment of Treason, but no Attainder of Treason shall work Corruption of Blood, or Forfeiture except during the Life of the Person attainted.

Article. IV.

Section. 1.

Full Faith and Credit shall be given in each State to the public Acts, Records, and judicial Proceedings of every other State. And the Congress may by general Laws prescribe the Manner in which such Acts, Records and Proceedings shall be proved, and the Effect thereof.

Section. 2.

The Citizens of each State shall be entitled to all Privileges and Immunities of Citizens in the several States.

A Person charged in any State with Treason, Felony, or other Crime, who shall flee from Justice, and be found in another State, shall on Demand of the executive Authority of the State from which he fled, be delivered up, to be removed to the State having Jurisdiction of the Crime.

No Person held to Service or Labour in one State, under the Laws thereof, escaping into another, shall, in Consequence of any Law or Regulation therein, be discharged from such Service or Labour, but shall be delivered up on Claim of the Party to whom such Service or Labour may be due.

Section. 3.

New States may be admitted by the Congress into this Union; but no new State shall be formed or erected within the Jurisdiction of any other State; nor any State be formed by the Junction of two or more States, or Parts of States, without the Consent of the Legislatures of the States concerned as well as of the Congress.

The Congress shall have Power to dispose of and make all needful Rules and Regulations respecting the Territory or other Property belonging to the United States; and nothing in this Constitution shall be so construed as to Prejudice any Claims of the United States, or of any particular State.

Section. 4.

The United States shall guarantee to every State in this Union a Republican Form of Government, and shall protect each of them against Invasion; and on Application of the Legislature, or of the Executive (when the Legislature cannot be convened), against domestic Violence.

Article. V.

The Congress, whenever two thirds of both Houses shall deem it necessary, shall propose Amendments to this Constitution, or, on the Application of the Legislatures of two thirds of the several States, shall call a Convention for proposing Amendments, which, in either Case, shall be valid to all Intents and Purposes, as Part of this Constitution, when ratified by the Legislatures of three fourths of the several States, or by Conventions in three fourths thereof, as the one or the other Mode of Ratification may be proposed by the Congress; Provided that no Amendment which may be made prior to the Year One thousand eight hundred and eight shall in any Manner affect the first and fourth Clauses in the Ninth Section of the first Article; and that no State, without its Consent, shall be deprived of its equal Suffrage in the Senate.

Article. VI.

All Debts contracted and Engagements entered into, before the Adoption of this Constitution, shall be as valid against the United States under this Constitution, as under the Confederation.

This Constitution, and the Laws of the United States which shall be made in Pursuance thereof;

and all Treaties made, or which shall be made, under the Authority of the United States, shall be the supreme Law of the Land; and the Judges in every State shall be bound thereby, any Thing in the Constitution or Laws of any State to the Contrary notwithstanding.

The Senators and Representatives before mentioned, and the Members of the several State Legislatures, and all executive and judicial Officers, both of the United States and of the several States, shall be bound by Oath or Affirmation, to support this Constitution; but no religious Test shall ever be required as a Qualification to any Office or public Trust under the United States.

Article. VII.

The Ratification of the Conventions of nine States, shall be sufficient for the Establishment of this Constitution between the States so ratifying the Same.

The Word, "the," being interlined between the seventh and eighth Lines of the first Page, the Word "Thirty" being partly written on an Erazure in the fifteenth Line of the first Page, The Words "is tried" being interlined between the thirty second and thirty third Lines of the first Page and the Word "the" being interlined between the forty third and forty fourth Lines of the second Page.

Attest William Jackson Secretary

Done in Convention by the Unanimous Consent of the States present the Seventeenth Day of September in the Year of our Lord one thousand seven hundred and Eighty seven and of the Independence of the United States of America the Twelfth In witness whereof We have hereunto subscribed our Names.

Appendix E • Presidential Gallery

Presidents and their terms in office

George Washington
1789-1797

James Madison
1809-1817

John Adams
1797-1801

James Monroe
1817-1825

Thomas Jefferson
1801-1809

John Quincy Adams
1825-1829

Andrew Jackson
<u>1829-1837</u>

John Tyler
<u>1841-1845</u>

**Martin
Van Buren**
<u>1837-1841</u>

James K. Polk
<u>1845-1849</u>

**William H.
Harrison**
<u>1841</u>

Zachary Taylor
<u>1849-1850</u>

 **Millard Fillmore**
1850-1853

 **Abraham Lincoln**
1861-1865

 **Franklin Pierce**
1853-1857

 **Andrew Johnson**
1865-1869

 **James Buchanan**
1857-1861

 **Ulysses S. Grant**
1869-1877

Rutherford B. Hayes
<u>1877-1881</u>

Grover Cleveland
<u>1885-1889</u>
<u>1893-1897</u>

James A. Garfield
<u>1881</u>

Benjamin Harrison
<u>1889-1893</u>

Chester A. Arthur
<u>1881-1885</u>

William McKinley
<u>1897-1901</u>

Theodore Roosevelt
<u>1901-1909</u>

Warren G. Harding
<u>1921-1923</u>

William H. Taft
<u>1909-1913</u>

Calvin Coolidge
<u>1923-1929</u>

Woodrow Wilson
<u>1913-1921</u>

Herbert C. Hoover
<u>1929-1933</u>

**Franklin Delano
Roosevelt**
1933-1945

**John F.
Kennedy**
1961-1963

**Harry S.
Truman**
1945-1953

**Lyndon B.
Johnson**
1963-1969

**Dwight D.
Eisenhower**
1953-1961

**Richard M.
Nixon**
1969-1974

Gerald R. Ford
1974-1977

George H. Bush
1989-1993

Jimmy Carter
1977-1981

William Clinton
1993-2001

Ronald W. Reagan
1981-1989

George W. Bush
2001-

CHAPTER ONE: page 6: *Lincoln Memorial*, Microsoft Corporation; page 8: *The Merchandise Of . . . Slaves, And Souls Of Men*, from "Africans on Board the Slave Bark *Wildfire*, April 30, 1860.", *Harper's Weekly*, June 2, 1860. Copyprint. Prints and Photographs Division, Library of Congress, Reproduction Number: LC-USZ62-19607 (1-20) ; page 11: Photo/caption from "Archiving Early America" - originally appearing in The American Gazetteer published by Jedidiah Morse in 1797, from "HISTORICAL MAPS FROM EARLY AMERICA" (http:\\earlyamerica.com); page 13: United States Political Map, National Geographic, © 1996 NGS Cartographic Division.

CHAPTER TWO: page 20: *Arlington National Cemetery*, Photodisk Inc.; page 22, *No stamped paper to be had. [Philadelphia : Printed by Hall & Franklin, 1765]*, Nov. 7, 1765, issue no. 1924, of the Pennsylvania gazette, printed at Philadelphia by David Hall and Benjamin Franklin; BOOK SOURCE: ap; vj14 06-15-98; 98-160405, Printed Ephemera Collection; Portfolio 346, Folder 45. Library of Congress, DIGITAL ID: rbpe 34604500 urn:hdl:loc.rbc/rbpe.34604500; page 23, *Cornwallis* (smaller photo) from Archiving Early America, (http://www.animus.net), all rights reserved, *Surrender of Lord Cornwallis* (larger) by Trumbull, John, 1756-1843, artist., from the Detroit Publishing Company Photograph Collection , REPOSITORY, Library of Congress Prints and Photographs Division Washington, D.C. 20540 USA, DIGITAL ID (original) det 4a31167 ; page 24, *"Original Rough Draught of the Declaration of Independence"* from the Library of Congress; page 27: *Sitting Bull (photo/caption)*, from The Little Bighorn Photo Gallery, Copyright ©1999 by Richard Federici - All rights reserved; page 28, *Mexican War Map*, (map/caption) Microsoft Corporation; page 31, *Fort Monroe, Va. Officers of 3d Pennsylvania Heavy Artillery*, from Selected Civil War photographs, 1861-1865 (Library of Congress) REPRODUCTION NUMBER LC-B8171-7486 DLC (b&w film neg.), Library of Congress Prints and Photographs Division Washington, D.C. 20540 USA, Digital ID: cwp 4a40120; page 32, *Auction and Negro Sales, Whitehall Street*, from Selected Civil War photographs, 1861-1865 (Library of Congress) REPRODUCTION NUMBER: LC-B8171-3608 DLC (b&w film neg.), REPOSITORY: Library of Congress Prints and Photographs Division Washington, D.C. 20540 USA, Digital ID (b&w film copy neg.): cwp 4a39949; page 33, *$200 reward*, Printed Ephemera Collection; Portfolio 86, Folder 2, COLLECTION: Broadsides, leaflets, and pamphlets from America and Europe, Digital ID: rbpe 08600200 urn:hdl:loc.rbc/rbpe; page 34, *Portrait of Maj. Gen. Ulysses S. Grant, officer of the Federal Army*, REPOSITORY: Library of Congress Prints and Photographs Division Washington, D.C. 20540 USA; Digital ID: 4a40423, *Portrait of Gen. Robert E. Lee, officer of the Confederate Army*, Washington, D.C. : Library of Congress, 1977. No. 1035 Forms part of Selected Civil War photographs, 1861-1865 (Library of Congress)

REPRODUCTION NUMBER: LC-B8172-0001 DLC (b&w film neg.) REPOSITORY: Library of Congress Prints and Photographs Division Washington, D.C. 20540 USA, Digital ID: cwp 4a40265; page 37, *District of Columbia. Company E, 4th U.S. Colored Infantry*, at Fort Lincoln, REPOSITORY Library of Congress Prints and Photographs Division Washington, D.C. 20540 USA, Digital ID: (b&w film copy neg.) cwp 4a40242, page 38: *The first reading of the Emancipation Proclamation before the cabinet*, painted by F.B. Carpenter ; engraved by A.H. Ritchie. REPRODUCTION NUMBER: LC-USZ62-2070 DLC (b&w film copy neg.) REPOSITORY: Library of Congress Prints and Photographs Division Washington, D.C. 20540 USA, Digital ID: cph 3a05802; page 39, *Theodore Roosevelt and the Rough Riders*, Library of Congress; page 41, *Spanish-American War Map*, (map/caption) Microsoft Corporation: page 42, William McKinley, Library of Congress; page 43, *US 7th Machine Gun Battalion, 3rd Division at Chateau Thierry bridgehead*, from Photos of the Great War - WWI Image Archive, http://www.ukans.edu/~kansite/ww_one/ photos/greatwar.htm; page 45, *Europe Before and After WWI*, Microsoft Corporation; page 46, Inauguration of President Wilson, second term, Copyright deposit; Jno. R. Idoux; March 16, 1917; DLC/PP-1917:45326. REPOSITORY: Library of Congress Prints and Photographs Division Washington, D.C. 20540 USA, Digital ID: pan 6a28173; page 48, *The Big Three*, REPRODUCTION NUMBER LC-USZ62-32833 DLC (b&w film copy neg.), REPOSITORY: Library of Congress Prints and Photographs Division Washington, D.C. 20540 USA, Digital ID: cph 3a33351; page 49, *Dwight Eisenhower*, REPRODUCTION NUMBER: LC-USZ62-25600 DLC (b&w film copy neg.) REPOSITORY: Library of Congress Prints and Photographs Division Washington, D.C. 20540 USA Digital ID: cph 3a26521; page 51, *Harry Truman*, Library of Congress; page 52, *General Douglas MacArthur*, from the MacArthur Memorial (http://sites.communitylink.org/mac/index.html); page 54, from the LBJ Digital Photo Archive.

CHAPTER THREE: page 60, *Mount Rushmore*, Photodisk Inc.; pages 62-66, Presidential portraits from the Library of Congress; page 67, *Md. Allan Pinkerton, President Lincoln, and Major Gen. John A. McClernand*, REPRODUCTION NUMBER: LC-B8171-7949 DLC (b&w film neg.) COLLECTION: Selected Civil War photographs, 1861-1865 (Library of Congress), REPOSITORY: Library of Congress Prints and Photographs Division Washington, D.C. 20540 USA, Digital ID: cwp 4a40264 ; page 68, *Ford Theatre*, Library of Congress; page 69, *Theodore Roosevelt*, REPRODUCTION NUMBER: LC-USZ62-13026 DLC , REPOSITORY: Library of Congress Prints and Photographs Division Washington, D.C. 20540 USA, Digital ID: cph 3a53299; page 70, *Theodore Roosevelt and John Muir*, REPRODUCTION NUMBER: LC-USZ62-107389 DLC (b&w film copy neg.) Digital ID:amrvp 3c07389; page 70, *Theodore Roosevelt, Library of Congress*; page 71, *Woodrow Wilson*, REPRODUCTION NUMBER: LC-USZ62-13028 DLC (b&w film copy neg. of cropped image)LC-USZ62-249 DLC (b&w film copy neg.) REPOSITORY: Library of Congress Prints and Photographs Division Washington, D.C.

20540 USA DIGITAL ID: (b&w film copy neg. of cropped image) cph 3a55007, (b&w film copy neg.) cph 3a04218, page 72, *Franklin D. Roosevelt*, REPRODUCTION NUMBER: LC-USZ62-117121 DLC (b&w film copy neg. of detail), LC-USZ62-26759 DLC (b&w film copy neg.), REPOSITORY: Library of Congress Prints and Photographs Division Washington, D.C. 20540 USA, DIGITAL ID: (b&w film copy neg. of detail) cph 3c17121, (b&w film copy neg.) cph 3a27556 ; page 73, *Roosevelt Signs War Declaration*, REPRODUCTION NUMBER: LC-USZ62-15185 DLC (b&w film copy neg.), REPOSITORY: Library of Congress Prints and Photographs Division Washington, D.C. 20540 USA, DIGITAL ID: cph 3a17434; page 74, *Roosevelt's Funeral*, REPRODUCTION NUMBER: LC-USZ62-67439 DLC (b&w film copy neg.), REPOSITORY: Library of Congress Prints and Photographs Division Washington, D.C. 20540 USA DIGITAL ID: cph 3b14914.

CHAPTER FOUR: Page 78, *Statue of Liberty,* Photodisk Inc.; page 80, *Signing the Declaration of Independence*, REPRODUCTION NUMBER: LC-H8-CT-C01-062-E DLC (color corrected film copy slide), COLLECTION: Theodor Horydczak Collection (Library of Congress), REPOSITORY: Library of Congress Prints and Photographs Division Washington, D.C. 20540 USA, DIGITAL ID: thc 5a51229; page 81, *Declaration of Independence*, engraved by W.L. Ormsby, REPRODUCTION NUMBER: LC-USZ62-3736 DLC (b&w film copy neg.), LC-USZ62-56 DLC (b&w film copy neg.), REPOSITORY: Library of Congress Prints and Photographs Division Washington, D.C. 20540 USA, DIGITAL ID: cph 3a07200; page 82, *Making the Flag*, REPRODUCTION NUMBER: LC-D416-90422 DLC (b&w glass neg.) COLLECTION: Detroit Publishing Company Photograph Collection, REPOSITORY: Library of Congress Prints and Photographs Division Washington, D.C. 20540 USA, DIGITAL ID: det 4a26653; page 83, *Civil Rights Act of 1964*, from the LBJ Digital Photo Archive; page 84, *Constitution of the United States*, from the National Archives and Records Administration; page 86, *Capitol Hill*, Microsoft Corporation; page 89, Kissinger, Nixon, Ford, Haig, from the Gerald Ford Library.

CHAPTER FIVE: page 96, *Washington Monument*, Washington Monument Photo Gallery; page 99, *Eisenhower*, REPRODUCTION NUMBER: LC-USZ62-84331 DLC (b&w film copy neg.) REPOSITORY: Library of Congress Prints and Photographs Division Washington, D.C. 20540 USA DIGITAL ID: cph 3b30902; page 100, *Johnson takes the Oath*, from the LBJ Digital Photo Archive, by Cecil Stoughton; page 101, *Robert Kennedy*, from the LBJ Digital Photo Archive, by Yoichi R. Okamoto; page 103, *Ronald Reagan* (source unknown), caption Microsoft Corporation; page 105, *Bill Clinton*, Michigan State University, caption Microsoft Corporation.

CHAPTER SIX: Page 112, *White House*, Microsoft Corporation; page 115, *Martin Luther King*, United Press; page 117, *Albert Einstein*, source unknown; page 119, *Susan B. Anthony*,